A GUIDE TO

THE MERCHANT OF VENICE

The Shakespeare Handbooks

Guides available now:

- Antony and Cleopatra
- As You Like It
- The Comedy of Errors
- Cymbeline
- Hamlet
- Henry IV, Part 1
- Julius Caesar
- King Lear
- Macbeth
- Measure for Measure
- The Merchant of Venice
- The Merry Wives of Windsor
- A Midsummer Night's Dream
- Much Ado About Nothing
- Othello
- Richard II
- Romeo and Juliet
- The Tempest
- Twelfth Night
- The Winter's Tale

Further titles in preparation.

The Shakespeare Handbooks

A Guide to
The Merchant of Venice

Alistair McCallum

Upstart Crow Publications

First published in 2018 by
Upstart Crow Publications

Copyright © Alistair McCallum 2018

A CIP catalogue record for this book
is available from the British Library

ISBN 978 1 899747 13 9

www.shakespeare-handbooks.com

Setting the scene

Shakespeare wrote *The Merchant of Venice* in or around 1597, when he was in his early thirties. For several years, he had been a member of London's leading theatre company, the Lord Chamberlain's Men, and already had a formidable reputation as a playwright; in particular, his recent plays *Romeo and Juliet* and *A Midsummer Night's Dream* had proved hugely popular.

The continuing success of *The Jew of Malta*, Christopher Marlowe's play of the early 1590s, may have influenced Shakespeare in his choice of subject-matter; however, in Shylock, the Jewish moneylender of *The Merchant of Venice*, Shakespeare created a far more complex, nuanced character than his counterpart in Marlowe's play. Although there had been virtually no Jews living in the country for hundreds of years, anti-Semitic sentiments were commonplace in Shakespeare's England. These feelings erupted when, in 1594, Queen Elizabeth's physician, Roderigo Lopez, a Portuguese Jew who had converted to Christianity, was suspected of attempting to poison the Queen; these events too may have influenced the creation of Shylock.

The presence of this outsider figure, together with the subject of moneylending – another highly charged topic of the day – and the threat of violent onstage revenge, placed as they are alongside the play's elements of traditional fairy-tale romantic comedy, can make *The Merchant of Venice* an uncomfortable work. However, this has not deterred generations of directors, actors, readers and critics from tackling the play, and it remains enduringly popular.

"The Merchant of Venice is a richly complicated work in which several themes are presented in the framework of a traditional comedy ... the play illustrates a theme that occupied Shakespeare in most of his comedies, the triumph of love over false and inhumane attitudes towards life."

Charles Boyce, *Shakespeare A to Z*, 1990

High stakes

The Republic of Venice is a busy, prosperous centre of international commerce. Majestic trading-ships from all over the world bring valuable, exotic goods to the city's port; and in the bustling commercial marketplace, merchants risk fortunes on shipping precious cargoes across the high seas.

One such merchant is Antonio, a wealthy Venetian. Renowned for his generosity, he is highly regarded, and has many friends in the city. He has invested heavily in several trading ventures, and stands to increase his wealth even further.

The outlook seems bright for Antonio. Something, however, appears to be troubling him; and his friends want to find out more.

Curtain up

A strange sadness

In conversation with his friends Salarino and Salanio, Antonio reveals that he is in low spirits. The origin of his melancholy, however, is a mystery to him:

> *Antonio:* In sooth[1] I know not why I am so sad.
> It wearies me; you say it wearies you;
> But how I caught it, found it or came by it,
> What stuff 'tis made of, whereof it is born,
> I am to learn[2] ...
>
> [1] *truth*
> [2] *I have not yet discovered, I do not know*

His two friends are in no doubt; it is Antonio's anxiety about his precious cargoes, now at sea, that is weighing on his mind. They would both feel exactly the same, they insist, if their wealth were at the mercy of the oceans:

> *Salanio:* Believe me, sir, had I such venture forth,[1]
> The better part of my affections would
> Be with my hopes abroad.[2] I should be still
> Plucking the grass to know where sits the wind,[3]
> Peering in maps for ports and piers and roads ...
>
> [1] *if I were involved in such risky enterprises*
> [2] *most of my thoughts and emotions would be
> with my merchandise out at sea*
> [3] *I would continually be scattering blades of grass
> to check the direction of the wind*

"For the new commercial civilizations of the Renaissance, wealth glowed in luminous metal, shone in silks, perfumed the air in spices ... the 1590s were a period when London was becoming conscious of itself as wealthy and cultivated, so that it could consider great commercial Venice as a prototype. And yet there were at the same time traditional suspicions of the profit motive and newly urgent anxieties about the power of money to disrupt human relations ..."

C. L. Barber, *The Merchants and the Jew of Venice*, 1959

Even in church, Salarino imagines, there can be no escape from the constant worry that everything could be lost in an instant:

> *Salarino:*   Should I go to church
> And see the holy edifice[1] of stone
> And not bethink me straight[2] of dangerous rocks,
> Which, touching but my gentle vessel's side,
> Would scatter all her spices on the stream,
> Enrobe[3] the roaring waters with my silks,
> And in a word, but even now worth this,
> And now worth nothing?[4]

> [1] *altar*
> [2] *immediately be reminded*
> [3] *cover, clothe*
> [4] *my valuable cargo would be rendered worthless
> from one moment to the next*

Antonio insists that he is not worried about his business ventures. He has a number of consignments in different ships, and is in no danger of losing everything in a single accident.

In that case there can only be one explanation, suggests Salanio: Antonio is in love. The young merchant denies it adamantly. His friends' attempts to tease him and cheer him up are interrupted as three more men arrive on the scene: Lorenzo, Gratiano, and Antonio's oldest friend Bassanio.

Salanio and Salarino leave, and Gratiano, the most talkative of the new arrivals, remarks at once on Antonio's air of dejection. Like the others, he assumes that Antonio is preoccupied with his business dealings, and warns him against spending all his time in a state of anxiety:

> *Gratiano:* You look not well, Signior Antonio;
> You have too much respect upon the world:[1]
> They lose it that do buy it with much care.[2]

> [1] *you pay too much attention to material concerns*
> [2] *people who worry too much about worldly
> matters are unable to enjoy the world's pleasures*

Antonio denies that he is excessively materialistic: perhaps it is simply his lot in life to be unhappy. Gratiano persists. Some people adopt a grave, calm demeanour, he claims, in the hope that they will be regarded as wise and profound. He urges Antonio not to put his well-being at risk by following their example:

> *Gratiano:* Why should a man whose blood is warm within
> Sit like his grandsire cut in alabaster? [1]
> Sleep when he wakes? And creep into the jaundice
> By being peevish?
>
> [1] *be still and lifeless, like the monument on the tomb of his dead grandfather*

Promising to continue with his lecture when they next meet, Gratiano takes his leave. Lorenzo, complaining that he can never get a word in edgeways in Gratiano's company, leaves with him.

A friend in need

Earlier, Bassanio had mentioned to Antonio that he was in love with a young lady, and had set his heart on marrying her. Now that the two men are alone, Antonio is keen to know more.

However, Bassanio does not answer his friend directly. Instead, he reminds Antonio of the precarious financial situation that he is in, freely admitting that he is the victim of his own extravagance:

> *Bassanio:* 'Tis not unknown to you, Antonio,
> How much I have disabled mine estate [1]
> By something showing a more swelling port
> Than my faint means would grant continuance. [2]
>
> [1] *used up my wealth*
> [2] *by displaying a rather more lavish lifestyle than my limited resources would allow*

Bassanio emphasises that he is not complaining about his situation or the more frugal life that he is now obliged to live. His only aim is to pay off his debts, and the greatest of these is to Antonio, who has been very generous to him.

Bassanio goes on to reveal that he has found a way to solve all his financial problems, and he wants his friend to be the first to know:

> *Bassanio:*   To you, Antonio,
> I owe the most in money and in love,
> And from your love I have a warranty
> To unburden[1] all my plots and purposes
> How to get clear of all the debts I owe.
>
> [1] *this love permits me to disclose*

Antonio immediately promises that he will help Bassanio in any way that he can. Bassanio, however, continues in a roundabout manner. He describes how, as a child, he would sometimes lose an arrow; the best way to find it, he recalls, was to shoot another in the same direction, keeping a close eye on it. In the same way, he implies, a further loan from Antonio may well lead to the recovery of all the money he has lent in the past.

Antonio responds impatiently. His love for Bassanio is such that no lengthy explanations or justifications are necessary; if he needs help, he should ask directly. Antonio will be offended, he declares, if Bassanio doubts his sincerity.

Bassanio now comes to the point. He is, as Antonio mentioned, in love, but money is also involved:

> *Bassanio:* In Belmont is a lady richly left,[1]
> And she is fair and, fairer than that word,
> Of wondrous virtues. Sometimes from her eyes
> I did receive fair speechless messages.
> Her name is Portia …
>
> [1] *in possession of a large inheritance*

Portia has many admirers. If Bassanio is to stand a chance of winning her hand in marriage, he needs to find enough money to match the prosperous bearing of her other suitors. The potential rewards, however, are huge:

Bassanio: ... her sunny locks
          Hang on her temples like a golden fleece ...
          ... many Jasons[1] come in quest of her.
          O my Antonio, had I but the means[2]
          To hold a rival place with one of them,
          I have a mind presages me such thrift
          That I should questionless be fortunate.[3]

> [1] *men hoping for success, like the mythological hero Jason in his quest for the Golden Fleece*
> [2] *money*
> [3] *I believe I will have such an advantage that I will undoubtedly end up rich and happy*

Antonio is keen to help. All his money is currently invested in merchandise, but he is confident that his good name in Venice is sufficient to secure a substantial loan. He urges Bassanio to raise whatever money he needs, and promises to act as his guarantor.

... her sunny locks
Hang on her temples like a golden fleece ...

In *The Merchant of Venice*, more than in any other play by Shakespeare, the themes of love and beauty are repeatedly intertwined with those of money and property:

"The value of Portia in Merchant of Venice *is measured in material terms. Because of her status as an heiress, she is a commodity, a golden fleece in a Venetian version of Jason's quest."*

Alison Findlay, *Women in Shakespeare*, 2014

A succession of admirers

At her home in Belmont, Portia is complaining to her waiting-woman Nerissa. Portia's father died recently, leaving her a considerable inheritance of money and property: however, his will also included instructions that prevent her from choosing her own husband.

Nerissa has little sympathy for her mistress, advising her to be content with her good fortune. Portia agrees that this would be a wise attitude, but insists that the theory and practice of wisdom are two different things. Sensible advice is often blithely ignored, particularly by the young and spirited:

> *Portia:* The brain may devise laws for the blood, but a hot temper leaps o'er a cold decree; such a hare is madness the youth, to skip o'er the meshes [1] of good counsel the cripple.

> [1] *nets, traps*

Even on the question of Portia's marriage, Nerissa refuses to commiserate, taking the side of her mistress's father:

> *Portia:* I may neither choose who I would, nor refuse who I dislike, so is the will of a living daughter curbed by the will of a dead father. Is it not hard, Nerissa, that I cannot choose one, nor refuse none?
> *Nerissa:* Your father was ever virtuous, and holy men at their death have good inspirations.

Nerissa now mentions the unconventional arrangement that Portia's father has made for her marriage. In order to gain Portia's hand, suitors will have to choose between three caskets, one of gold, one of silver, and one of lead. Nerissa is confident that, however strange the procedure might seem, it will produce the right husband for Portia.

Portia now describes the suitors she has already encountered. They are all, in their different ways, totally unsuitable. The first, a Prince of Naples, was obsessed with his horse:

Portia: Ay, that's a colt [1] indeed, for he doth nothing but talk of his horse ... I am much afeard my lady his mother played false with a smith. [2]

> [1] *inexperienced, impulsive youth*
> [2] *had an affair with a blacksmith*

The next, a central European Count, was unbearably sombre and humourless. He was followed by a Frenchman who, by contrast, was wild and unpredictable. An Englishman came next. Although he was handsome, language proved an insurmountable barrier:

Nerissa: What say you then to Falconbridge, the young baron of England?

Portia: You know I say nothing to him, for he understands not me, nor I him. He hath neither Latin, French nor Italian ... He is a proper man's picture, [1] but, alas, who can converse with a dumb-show?

> [1] *in terms of good looks, he is the ideal man*

To make matters worse, the baron had strange, confused dress sense, having apparently obtained his clothes from a variety of countries; and he became involved in a violent scuffle with the Scottish lord who arrived at the same time.

Finally Nerissa mentions the German suitor. Portia, appalled at the young man's drinking, shudders at the thought of him:

Nerissa: How like you the young German, the Duke of Saxony's nephew?

Portia: Very vilely in the morning, when he is sober, and most vilely in the afternoon, when he is drunk. When he is best, he is a little worse than a man, and when he is worst he is little better than a beast.

Nerissa reassures Portia that all the suitors she has seen so far are due to return home without undertaking the task of choosing the correct casket. Portia is greatly relieved:

> *Portia:* I am glad this parcel of wooers are so reasonable, for there is not one among them but I dote on his very absence, and I pray God grant them a fair departure.

Nerissa mentions that another gentleman, a Venetian, visited Belmont when Portia's father was still alive: he was a far more suitable match, in her opinion, than any of her recent suitors. Portia remembers the man, and recollects that his name was Bassanio. However, before they can pursue the subject further, a servant enters: he announces that yet another suitor, the Prince of Morocco, is on his way.

"When we meet Portia in Belmont we see that although she is a noble or patrician woman with wealth and status, she is also imprisoned by her father's decree that whichever suitor passes the casket test shall marry her. Shakespeare presents marriage metaphorically as a form of containment and trafficking of women, specifically within aristocratic circles; in this case, a daughter is being controlled from the grave."

Farah Karim-Cooper, *Questions of Value in* The Merchant of Venice, 2016

An uncomfortable meeting

Back in Venice, Bassanio is in search of a loan. He is talking to Shylock, a Jewish moneylender, and has asked for three thousand ducats, to be repaid within three months.

Shylock, taking his time, mulls over Bassanio's request. Bassanio has explained that the merchant Antonio will be guarantor for the repayment of the loan. Shylock suggests that there might be cause for concern:

Bassanio: ... Shall I know your answer?
Shylock: Three thousand ducats for three months, and Antonio bound.[1]
Bassanio: Your answer to that.
Shylock: Antonio is a good man.
Bassanio: Have you heard any imputation to the contrary?
Shylock: Ho, no, no, no, no. My meaning in saying he is a good man is to have you understand me that he is sufficient,[2] yet his means are in supposition.[3] He hath an argosy[4] bound to Tripoli, another to the Indies ...

[1] *responsible, liable*
[2] *wealthy enough to provide security*
[3] *uncertain, at risk*
[4] *large merchant ship*

Shylock dwells for a while on the dangers of carrying goods by sea. Finally, however, he declares that he is prepared to lend Bassanio the money. He wishes to talk first to Antonio about guaranteeing the loan, and Bassanio asks him to join them for a meal. Shylock is dismissive:

Shylock: Yes, to smell pork, to eat of the habitation which your prophet the Nazarite conjured the devil into.[1] I will buy with you, sell with you, talk with you, walk with you and so following. But I will not eat with you, drink with you nor pray with you.

[1] *Jesus was reputed to have driven demons from a possessed man into a herd of swine*

At this point Antonio himself arrives. Shylock knows him, and in an aside reveals that he despises the merchant:

Shylock: How like a fawning publican[1] he looks.
I hate him for he is a Christian;
But more, for that in low simplicity
He lends out money gratis,[2] and brings down
The rate of usance[3] here with us in Venice.

[1] *public official, tax collector; lackey*
[2] *because, in his naivety, he lends money freely*
[3] *interest, return*

Usury – the lending of money at interest – was a hugely controversial subject in Elizabethan England. There was a widespread sentiment (backed up by scripture) that charging interest was immoral, along with a sense of nostalgia for an imagined past when money was lent freely between friends. At the same time, however, moneylending at high rates of interest was rife, and was a frequent cause of bankruptcy and misery at all levels of society.

Usury was made legal in 1571, when the law permitted lenders to charge a maximum of ten percent interest. However, unofficial moneylending at higher rates continued; Shakespeare's father, for example, was prosecuted twice for this offence. Legal or not, the practice was generally frowned on:

"For the Elizabethans, in transition from feudalism to a mercantile, capitalist economy, usury was a living issue of debate ... Merchants needed credit for their trading. So did actors – Shakespeare's company, the Chamberlain's Men, built the Globe with money borrowed at interest and repaid with difficulty ... Usury was tolerated with distaste; the usurer was reviled."

John Goodwin, Royal Shakespeare Company programme notes, 1965

Antonio, in turn, despises the Jews, and frequently disparages them in public. If Shylock can find an opportunity for revenge, he is determined to take it.

Shylock explains to Bassanio that he does not have the full amount to hand, but will easily be able to obtain what he needs from one of his fellow Jews. Pretending to notice Antonio for the first time, he greets him politely. Antonio responds cautiously, emphasising that he would never normally become involved with usury:

> *Shylock:* ... Rest you fair,[1] good signior,
> Your worship was the last man in our mouths.[2]
> *Antonio:* Shylock, albeit I neither lend nor borrow
> By taking nor by giving of excess,[3]
> Yet, to supply the ripe wants[4] of my friend,
> I'll break a custom.
>
> [1] *welcome, make yourself at home*
> [2] *we were just talking about you*
> [3] *interest*
> [4] *urgent needs*

Shylock defends the practice of charging interest, quoting the Old Testament story of Jacob, who profited as a shepherd from his astuteness and knowledge of sheep-breeding. Antonio is unmoved, and remarks to his friend that this demonstrates the Jew's wicked nature:

> *Antonio:* Mark you this, Bassanio,
> The devil can cite Scripture for his purpose.
> An evil soul producing holy witness
> Is like a villain with a smiling cheek,
> A goodly[1] apple, rotten at the heart.
> O, what a goodly outside falsehood hath!
>
> [1] *fine, attractive*

In the 1970s, a copy of the complete works of Shakespeare was smuggled into the prison on South Africa's Robben Island, which held many political prisoners including Nelson Mandela. The book, which became known as the 'Robben Island Bible', was passed around secretly from cell to cell, and many prisoners underlined passages in the text that they found particularly significant.

The anti-apartheid activist and senior African National Congress member Walter Sisulu, who was imprisoned on Robben Island for over twenty-five years, chose one of Shylock's speeches from *The Merchant of Venice*:

> *Still have I borne it with a patient shrug,*
> *For sufferance is the badge of all our tribe.*

Shylock's proposal

Antonio asks for confirmation that Shylock will indeed lend the money. Before answering, Shylock reminds him of the mistreatment he has suffered at Antonio's hands, often in the Rialto, Venice's public meeting-place for the city's merchants:

Shylock: Signior Antonio, many a time and oft
In the Rialto you have rated[1] me
About my moneys and my usances.[2]
Still have I borne it with a patient shrug,
For sufferance[3] is the badge of all our tribe.
You call me misbeliever, cut-throat dog,
And spit upon my Jewish gaberdine[4] …

[1] *criticised, reviled*
[2] *the interest I charge*
[3] *endurance, tolerance of oppression*
[4] *cloak*

Shylock questions whether it is fitting to lend money in the circumstances. Antonio replies, defiantly, that he will not change his views or his behaviour. He does not want the money as a gesture of friendship. In fact it would be to Shylock's advantage to think of him as a foe, in case the debt is not repaid:

> Antonio: ... lend it rather to thine enemy,
> Who, if he break,[1] thou mayst with better face[2]
> Exact the penalty.
>
> [1] *breaks his word; fails to repay*
> [2] *justification*

The mood changes suddenly as Shylock assures the men that he wishes to be on friendly terms with them, and to forget about past insults. To their surprise, he offers to lend them the money without demanding any interest at all. Instead he suggests that, as a joke, they include an unusual clause in their agreement:

> Shylock: Go with me to a notary,[1] seal me[2] there
> Your single bond,[3] and, in a merry sport,
> If you repay me not on such a day,
> In such a place, such sum, or sums, as are
> Expressed in the condition, let the forfeit
> Be nominated for an equal[4] pound
> Of your fair flesh, to be cut off and taken
> In what part of your body pleaseth me.
>
> [1] *official with the authority to draw up contracts*
> [2] *agree, put your hand to*
> [3] *simple promise to repay*
> [4] *just; exact*

Antonio immediately accepts the offer. His friend is unwilling to go along with the idea, but Antonio persuades him that repayment will not be a problem. He will soon be in possession of enough valuable merchandise to pay the debt many times over, so the threat of removing a pound of flesh is irrelevant:

> Antonio: Content, in faith: I'll seal to such a bond
> And say there is much kindness in the Jew.

Bassanio: You shall not seal to such a bond for me;
I'll rather dwell in my necessity.[1]
Antonio: Why, fear not, man, I will not forfeit it;
Within these two months, that's a month before
This bond expires, I do expect return
Of thrice three times the value of this bond.

[1] *I would prefer to continue living in financial
hardship*

Shylock insists that his offer is valid and benevolent. The penalty clause is just a joke; even if the debt were not repaid, what good would a pound of human flesh be to him in reality? Antonio agrees to guarantee the loan, and Shylock sets off to obtain the money. The three of them are to meet again shortly at the notary's office.

Antonio is delighted at the agreement, but Bassanio remains wary. However appealing the offer may be, he is convinced that the Jew is inherently untrustworthy:

Antonio: The Hebrew will turn Christian, he grows kind.
Bassanio: I like not fair terms and a villain's mind.

The figure of the villainous moneylender was a familiar one to an Elizabethan audience. Unlike Shylock, however, the typical usurer would not have been Jewish; there had been very few practising Jews in England for almost three hundred years, since their expulsion from the country in 1290.

"Shakespeare was not drawing from life in the 1590s when he created his memorable Jewish moneylender, Shylock ... since their banishment in the thirteenth century there had been no Jews living publicly in England, although historians have found evidence of a small, secret community in Elizabethan London. But Shylock, although he is present in only five scenes of the play, has become its most prominent character, with a cultural presence towering over his role in the plot."

Laurie Maguire and Emma Smith, *30 Great Myths about Shakespeare*, 2013

Portia sets out the rules

The Prince of Morocco has come to visit Portia, hoping to win her hand in marriage. She must not be deterred by his dark skin, he declares; his blood is as red as any man's, and in his own country his appearance inspires fear in brave men and love in young women.

Portia replies that she is not solely influenced by looks; in any case, she cannot make her own choice, but must abide by the result of the test set by her father for all prospective husbands. If this were not the case, she assures him, she would look on him every bit as favourably as any of her previous suitors.

The Prince thanks her, and asks to be taken to the room where the three caskets are. He proclaims that, as a fearless warrior, he would do anything to have Portia as his wife: however, he is concerned that the element of chance may mean that a lesser man is successful.

Portia reminds him of the conditions set by her father. He must choose between three caskets. If he chooses the correct one, he will marry Portia; if not, he must remain unmarried for the rest of his life.

> *Portia:*   You must take your chance,
> And either not attempt to choose at all,
> Or swear, before you choose, if you choose wrong
> Never to speak to lady afterward
> In way of marriage;[1] therefore be advised.[2]

[1] *never to make another proposal of marriage*
[2] *be warned; think carefully*

The Prince decides to take the challenge.

An eccentric reunion

Alone in the street, Lancelot Gobbo is having a confused but animated discussion with himself. He is currently Shylock's servant, but is on the verge of abandoning his employer. His virtuous conscience is telling him to stay, but the devil in his imagination is urging him to follow his desires and run away. Eventually the devil gains the upper hand:

Lancelot: 'Budge,' says the fiend. 'Budge not,' says my
conscience ... To be ruled by my conscience,
I should stay with the Jew my master, who, God
bless the mark,[1] is a kind of devil; and, to run away
from the Jew, I should be ruled by the fiend, who,
saving your reverence,[2] is the devil himself.
Certainly the Jew is the very devil incarnation, and,
in my conscience, my conscience is but a kind of
hard conscience, to offer to counsel me to stay with
the Jew. The fiend gives the more friendly counsel:
I will run, fiend, my heels are at your commandment;
I will run.

[1] *forgive the expression*
[2] *excuse me for saying so*

At this moment Gobbo's father appears. His eyesight is poor, and he does not recognise his long-lost son. The old man asks the way to Shylock's house, and Lancelot gives him a deliberately perplexing answer:

Old Gobbo: Master young gentleman, I pray you, which is
the way to Master Jew's?
Lancelot: Turn up on your right hand at the next turning, but,
at the next turning of all, on your left. Marry, at the
very next turning, turn of no hand, but turn down
indirectly to the Jew's house.
Old Gobbo: By God's sonties,[1] 'twill be a hard way to hit.[2]

[1] *saints*
[2] *it won't be easy to find*

Old Gobbo mentions that he is hoping to see his son, who works at the Jew's house. Lancelot decides to bewilder his father even more:

> *Lancelot:* … the young gentleman, according to Fates and Destinies and such odd sayings, the Sisters Three and such branches of learning, is indeed deceased, or, as you would say in plain terms, gone to heaven.

The old man is distraught; he was hoping that his son would support him in his old age. Lancelot continues to tease him:

> *Lancelot:* Do you not know me, father?
> *Old Gobbo:* Alack, sir, I am sand-blind,[1] I know you not.
> *Lancelot:* Nay, indeed, if you had your eyes you might fail of the knowing me: it is a wise father that knows his own child.

> [1] *partially blind*

Eventually Lancelot persuades the old man that he is indeed his son. Old Gobbo has brought a present for Shylock, but Lancelot explains that he has just decided to leave the Jew's service: his master never gave him enough to eat, he complains. Lancelot is aiming to find a new master, and the man he has in mind is Bassanio, whose servants are always supplied with smart new uniforms.

> *"It is not impossible that Shakespeare visited Venice, but it is unlikely. Yet a great port like London would have been full of travellers' tales. The Gobbo was a grotesque statue of a hunchback which supported a column from which heralds made announcements. It was the custom to place there verses satirising important figures in the city. It was an important mouthpiece of Venetian opinion, as are the cryptic observations of Shylock's servant, Lancelot Gobbo."*
>
> Nicholas Fogg, *Hidden Shakespeare*, 2013

Lancelot's wish is granted

By coincidence, Bassanio is passing at this very moment, busily giving orders to his attendants. He is preparing for a feast this evening to celebrate his imminent departure to Belmont, where he hopes to win Portia's hand.

Lancelot and his father approach Bassanio hesitantly and, in a convoluted manner, ask him whether there might be a job for Lancelot in his household:

Bassanio: ... Wouldst thou aught[1] with me?
Old Gobbo: Here's my son, sir, a poor boy –
Lancelot: Not a poor boy, sir, but the rich Jew's man that
would, sir, as my father shall specify –
Old Gobbo: He hath a great infection, sir, as one would
say, to serve.

[1] *do you want anything*

Eventually Bassanio cuts short the conversation. He knows that Lancelot Gobbo has been a worthy servant to Shylock, he says briskly, and is glad to have him as one of his own attendants.

Bassanio sends Lancelot off to take his leave of Shylock and to report for work at his new master's house, where he will be given a fine uniform. Lancelot is delighted. As he leaves, he boasts to his father of his good fortune. Looking at his palm, he proudly declares that he has an eventful life ahead of him:

Lancelot: Go to, here's a simple line of life;[1] here's a small
trifle of wives ... and then to scape drowning thrice,
and to be in peril of my life with the edge of a
feather-bed.[2]

[1] *an unbroken lifeline (on my palm)*
[2] *almost be killed by a jealous husband*

Gratiano now arrives. He has a favour to ask, and Bassanio, unable to refuse his friend anything, agrees before he has even heard the request. However, Bassanio is taken aback when he hears that Gratiano wishes to accompany him on his mission to Belmont. He is aware that his friend's manners may seem a little boisterous to those who do not know him well:

Gratiano: I have suit[1] to you.
Bassanio: You have obtained it.
Gratiano: You must not deny me; I must go with you to
        Belmont.
Bassanio: Why then, you must. But hear thee, Gratiano,
        Thou art too wild, too rude and bold of voice:
        Parts that become thee[2] happily enough
        And in such eyes as ours appear not faults.
        But where thou art not known, why, there they show
        Something too liberal.[3]

[1] *a request*
[2] *qualities that suit you*
[3] *they appear rather too undisciplined*

Gratiano must be on his best behaviour during their visit to Belmont; otherwise his friend's rowdiness could ruin Bassanio's chances of winning Portia. Gratiano promises to control himself once they arrive. They both agree, however, that tonight's feast at Bassanio's house is a different matter.

Jessica longs to escape
II, iii

Lancelot has returned briefly to Shylock's house before moving permanently to his new job. Shylock's daughter Jessica is sad to see him go:

Jessica: I am sorry thou wilt leave my father so.
        Our house is hell and thou, a merry devil,
        Didst rob it of some taste[1] of tediousness.

[1] *morsel, fragment*

She gives Lancelot a letter which he is to hand, secretly, to Bassanio's friend Lorenzo at the feast tonight. Lancelot says a fond farewell and leaves for Bassanio's house.

Alone, Jessica reveals how she is torn between her sense of duty and her rejection of her father and his values. Her planned future with Lorenzo will, she hopes, bring an end to her distress:

> *Jessica:*   … what heinous sin is it in me
> To be ashamed to be my father's child!
> But, though I am a daughter to his blood,
> I am not to his manners.[1] O, Lorenzo,
> If thou keep promise I shall end this strife,
> Become a Christian, and thy loving wife.

> [1] *character, behaviour*

An elopement is planned II, iv

Lorenzo and his friends are planning to slip away from the feast at some point this evening and return in disguise. Gratiano is concerned that they are not prepared; and as Salarino points out, they have not yet found a page-boy to carry the torch for them, as is traditional.

The discussion is interrupted by the arrival of Lancelot Gobbo, who hands Jessica's note to Lorenzo. His reaction immediately gives away the nature of the letter:

> *Lorenzo:* I know the hand;[1] in faith, 'tis a fair hand,
> And whiter than the paper it writ on
> Is the fair hand that writ.
> *Gratiano:*   Love news, in faith!

> [1] *handwriting*

Lancelot mentions that he is due to return to Jessica's house, as Bassanio has asked him to invite Shylock to the feast. Handing the servant some money, Lorenzo asks him to take a message to Jessica. He remarks enigmatically to his friends that they no longer need to look for a torch-carrier for this evening's festivities:

> *Lorenzo:*   Tell gentle Jessica
> I will not fail her; speak it privately.
> Go, gentlemen,
> Will you prepare you for this masque [1] tonight?
> I am provided of [2] a torch-bearer.
>
> [1] *our masked, disguised entrance at the feast*
> [2] *I have found*

Salarino and Salanio leave to carry on with their preparations for the feast. Lorenzo then confirms that, as Gratiano suspected, the letter was from Jessica. It explains how Lorenzo is to help her escape from her father's house, carrying plenty of money and jewels with her. To avoid arousing suspicion, she will be disguised as a page-boy; and she will carry the torch for Lorenzo and his friends when they make their dramatic appearance at the feast.

> *"The characters repeatedly find themselves forced to choose between conflicting obligations. Indeed, the central dramatic episodes all portray moments of choice ... The one characteristic which all these situations share in common is that they admit of no wholly satisfactory solution. So frequently is this idea repeated that Shakespeare seems to assume that insoluble dilemmas and unavoidable betrayals are an inescapable part of the human condition ..."*
>
> John Wilders, BBC TV Shakespeare edition
> of *The Merchant of Venice*, 1980

Shylock makes a decision

Back at Shylock's house, Lancelot's old master is warning him that he will find life with Bassanio a lot less comfortable. He calls out for his daughter, and tells her that he has been invited to Bassanio's house. He is in two minds about accepting the invitation, and is not impressed by Lancelot's confused attempt to persuade him:

Shylock: I am bid forth to supper, Jessica.
There are my keys. But wherefore [1] should I go?
I am not bid for love; they flatter me,
But yet I'll go in hate, to feed upon
The prodigal [2] Christian. Jessica, my girl,
Look to [3] my house. I am right loath to go …
Lancelot: I beseech you, sir, go. My young master doth expect your reproach. [4]
Shylock: So do I his.

[1] *why*
[2] *extravagant, overindulgent*
[3] *look after*
[4] *meaning 'approach'*

When Lancelot mentions that some young men may attend the feast in costumes and masks, Shylock is alarmed. He does not want his daughter to be exposed to such folly, and instructs her not to watch any such processions:

Shylock: What, are there masques? Hear you me, Jessica,
Lock up my doors, and when you hear the drum
And the vile squealing of the wry-necked fife, [1]
Clamber not you up to the casements [2] then,
Nor thrust your head into the public street
To gaze on Christian fools with varnished faces …

[1] *the flute-player with his contorted neck*
[2] *don't climb up to look out of the windows*

Eventually Shylock decides to attend the feast, and tells Lancelot to go ahead of him and give Bassanio his reply. As he is leaving, the servant furtively passes on Lorenzo's message to Jessica:

Lancelot: Mistress, look out at window for all this;[1]
There will come a Christian by
Will be worth a Jewess' eye.

[1] *despite what your father says*

When her father enquires, Jessica denies that the servant has said anything of importance. Shylock reflects that, on the whole, he is glad to be rid of Lancelot. With luck, he will help his new master Bassanio to get through his loan more quickly:

Shylock: The patch[1] is kind enough, but a huge feeder,
Snail-slow in profit,[2] and he sleeps by day
More than the wildcat. Drones[3] hive not with me,
Therefore I part with him, and part with him
To one that I would have him help to waste
His borrowed purse.

[1] *fool, clown*
[2] *in learning anything useful*
[3] *male bees who do no work*

As Shylock leaves, he urges his daughter once again to keep herself locked safely in the house. Alone, Jessica observes that the situation is not as secure as he imagines:

Jessica: Farewell, and if my fortune be not crossed,[1]
I have a father, you a daughter, lost.

[1] *if my luck holds; if nothing upsets my plans*

A sudden change of plan

Gratiano and Salarino, in their disguises, are waiting outside Shylock's house, as instructed by Lorenzo. To his friends' surprise, Lorenzo himself has not arrived yet. Those who have recently fallen in love, says Gratiano, are usually in a hurry to be united. This eagerness never lasts, he reflects cynically:

> *Gratiano:*   … who riseth from a feast
> With that keen appetite that he sits down?
> Where is the horse that doth untread again
> His tedious measures with the unbated fire [1]
> That he did pace them first? All things that are,
> Are with more spirit chased than enjoyed.
>
> [1] *retrace his wearying steps with the same undiminished energy*

Lorenzo finally hurries onto the scene, apologising profusely for his lateness, and immediately calls out to see who is at home. Jessica appears at an upstairs window, dressed as a page-boy, and the two lovers greet one another fondly.

Jessica hands down a casket full of valuables that she intends to take with her. She is unsure about carrying the torch for Lorenzo and his friends, as she wishes to attract as little attention as possible, but Lorenzo reassures her that no one will recognise her in her page's uniform. Pausing only to gather more of her father's gold, she climbs down from the window.

The friends set off for Bassanio's feast, Jessica lighting their way. Gratiano lingers for a moment, and at this point Bassanio's friend Antonio rushes in. He has some urgent news, and has been looking for them everywhere.

There is no time for their fancy dress antics, he insists; the feast is over. The wind has suddenly changed, and Bassanio is about to set sail for Belmont.

Gratiano, keen to accompany his friend on the journey, is not disappointed at the news:

Antonio: No masque tonight, the wind is come about.[1]
Bassanio presently will go aboard;
I have sent twenty out to seek for you.
Gratiano: I am glad on't. I desire no more delight
Than to be under sail and gone tonight.

[1] *has changed direction*

"*Shakespeare makes use of two distinct settings for* The Merchant of Venice. *Venice, as in Shakespeare's time, is the city of commerce where wealth flows in and out with each visiting ship. Venice is also a cosmopolitan city at the frontier of Christendom, beyond which lies Asia, Africa, and the Ottoman Empire. Society in Venice is a predominantly male world, where the single female, Jessica, is locked up in her house, and can only escape in disguise as a male.*

"*Belmont, on the other hand, is the home of Portia and her mysterious caskets. It is a place of romance and festivity ... Belmont is an idealized 'green world' that is removed from the ruthlessness of the real world. Unlike Venice, it is controlled by women (though Portia's dead father lingers).*"

Michael Best, *Venice and Belmont*, 2011

Gold, silver or lead?

The Prince of Morocco has decided to take the test set by Portia's father. A curtain is pulled back to reveal three caskets: if the Prince chooses the correct one, Portia will be his. On each casket there is an inscription. The Prince reads each one in turn, but the messages are far from clear:

Morocco: This first of gold, who this inscription bears:
'Who chooseth me shall gain what many men desire.'
The second, silver, which this promise carries:
'Who chooseth me shall get as much as he deserves.'
This third, dull lead, with warning all as blunt:
'Who chooseth me must give and hazard [1] all he hath.'
How shall I know if I do choose the right?
Portia: The one of them contains my picture, prince.
If you choose that, then I am yours withal. [2]
Morocco: Some god direct my judgement!

[1] *risk, venture*
[2] *I am yours along with the picture*

The Prince first considers the lead casket, but rejects it as beneath him. It makes no sense to chance everything on an object of no value:

Morocco: … men that hazard all
Do it in hope of fair advantages.
A golden mind stoops not to shows of dross; [1]
I'll then nor [2] give nor hazard aught [3] for lead.

[1] *worthless appearances*
[2] *neither*
[3] *anything*

The silver casket is more hopeful; it promises him what he deserves, and surely he deserves Portia? His personal qualities, his wealth and status, and the sheer strength of his love for her all make him a worthy husband.

For a moment he considers choosing the silver casket, but the inscription on the gold one is even more compelling:

Morocco: What if I strayed no farther, but chose here? [1]
            Let's see once more this saying graved in gold: [2]
            'Who chooseth me shall gain what many men desire.'
            Why, that's the lady; all the world desires her.
            From the four corners of the earth they come ...

[1] *the silver casket*
[2] *engraved on the gold casket*

The Prince agonises over his decision, but eventually makes up his mind. The gold casket is the only one worthy of containing Portia's picture; using any lesser metal would be blasphemy. Portia hands him the key.

To the Prince's horror, the casket contains a skull. In the eye-socket is a scroll, which he reads:

All that glisters is not gold,
Often have you heard that told.
Many a man his life hath sold
But my outside to behold. [1]
... Had you been as wise as bold,
Young in limbs, in judgement old, [2]
Your answer had not been inscrolled, [3]
Fare you well, your suit is cold. [4]

[1] *only because they were tempted by the superficial gleam of gold*
[2] *if you were as wise as you are bold, and had a mature mind in a young body*
[3] *you would not be reading this scroll; you would not have chosen this casket*
[4] *your petition is dead; your quest is over*

Stunned and desolate, the Prince can hardly speak. He says a brief, sad farewell, and leaves Belmont for ever.

Was the Prince of Morocco to reappear as a major tragic figure later in Shakespeare's career?

"Shakespeare, with evident nervousness, hurries Morocco through ... But this proud Moor, with his kingly presence and the swelling music of his speech, stays in our minds ... What would have happened if the story had suddenly become real? If Portia had fallen in love with Morocco and married him? How would the Venetians have reacted to him, and he to them? Othello *is precisely that story ..."*

John Wain, *The Living World of Shakespeare*, 1964

The mood darkens   II, viii

In a street in Venice, Salarino and Salanio are discussing the latest news. Bassanio has left for Belmont, as planned, and Gratiano is with him. As for Shylock, he is incensed that his daughter has eloped.

Convinced that Lorenzo and Jessica were on the ship with Bassanio, Shylock enlisted the help of the Duke of Venice himself, who agreed to assist personally in a search of the vessel; however, the ship had already sailed by the time they arrived. At the port, a rumour was heard that the young lovers had been spotted in a gondola, but no one knows where they are. The merchant Antonio has attested that they were not travelling with Bassanio.

Beside himself with rage, Shylock has been wandering the streets, crying out for justice, and bewailing the loss of his daughter, his money, and his jewels. He has become a figure of fun, attracting a crowd of children who mimic his anguished cries.

Salanio mentions that the moneylender will be in no mood to show mercy to Antonio if he cannot repay Bassanio's loan as agreed. Shylock is bound to associate Antonio with his terrible loss, even if the merchant was not directly involved.

The mention of Antonio reminds Salarino of a worrying report that he has just heard. It concerned the wreck of a Venetian ship in the English Channel:

> *Salanio:* Let good Antonio look he keep his day,[1]
> Or he shall pay for this.
> *Salarino:* Marry, well remembered.
> I reasoned[2] with a Frenchman yesterday
> Who told me, in the narrow seas that part
> The French and English, there miscarried[3]
> A vessel of our country richly fraught.[4]
> I thought upon Antonio when he told me …
>
> [1] *make sure that he repays by the agreed date*
> [2] *conversed*
> [3] *came to grief, went down*
> [4] *loaded with a valuable cargo*

Salarino hopes that the vessel is not one of Antonio's. Salanio advises him to tell Antonio of the accident, but to break the news to him gently in case he should find it upsetting.

They both agree that Antonio is a kind, considerate individual. When Bassanio was leaving for Belmont, says Salarino, Antonio urged him not to think about the money he had borrowed, but to take his time and to enjoy his romantic adventure. Antonio could hardly hide his tears as his friend departed. They will find the young man, they decide, and see if they can do anything to lift his spirits:

> *Salarino:* … with affection wondrous sensible,[1]
> He wrung Bassanio's hand, and so they parted.
> *Salanio:* I think he only loves the world for him.[2]
> I pray thee, let us go and find him out,
> And quicken his embraced heaviness[3]
> With some delight or other.
>
> [1] *wonderfully sensitive*
> [2] *Antonio only enjoys life because of Bassanio*
> [3] *enliven the troubled mood that has resulted from his own generosity*

An overconfident challenger

Another suitor has come to Belmont. This time it is a Spaniard, the Prince of Arragon, who is hoping to succeed. Aware of the rules, he surveys the three caskets carefully:

> *Arragon:* I am enjoined [1] by oath to observe three things:
> First, never to unfold [2] to anyone
> Which casket 'twas I chose; next, if I fail
> Of the right casket, never in my life
> To woo a maid in way of marriage;
> Lastly, if I do fail in fortune of my choice,
> Immediately to leave you and be gone.

> [1] *bound, committed*
> [2] *reveal*

Like the previous suitor, he takes his time, musing over the inscription on each casket. He rejects the lead casket out of hand, refusing to take a risk for such a dull object:

> *Arragon:* 'Who chooseth me must give and hazard all he hath.'
> You shall look fairer ere I give or hazard. [1]

> [1] *you (the casket) would have to look more
> attractive before I would take a chance for you*

He turns to the gold casket, but again the inscription does not appeal to him. He does not wish to be associated with the mass of common people, whose tastes are uneducated and superficial:

> *Arragon:* 'Who chooseth me shall gain what many men desire.'
> 'What many men desire': that 'many' may be meant
> By [1] the fool multitude that choose by show, [2]
> Not learning more than the fond [3] eye doth teach …

> [1] *may refer to*
> [2] *base their choices on outward appearances*
> [3] *foolish, easily influenced*

The message on the silver casket is much more to his liking. People should be rewarded according to their merit, he believes:

> *Arragon:* 'Who chooseth me shall get as much as he deserves.'
> And well said too; for who shall go about
> To cozen Fortune[1] and be honourable
> Without the stamp of merit?[2] Let none presume
> To wear an undeserved dignity.[3]
>
> [1] *who will try to outwit the forces of destiny*
> [2] *gain honour which is not justified by worth*
> [3] *no one should claim a status that they do not deserve*

Warming to his theme, the Prince denounces the corruption that enables unworthy individuals to prosper, often at the expense of those who are more deserving:

> *Arragon:* O, that estates, degrees and offices[1]
> Were not derived[2] corruptly …
> How many then should cover that stand bare?[3]
> How many be commanded that command?[4]
>
> [1] *if only social and official positions*
> [2] *gained*
> [3] *would not need to doff their hats, as they do now, to their supposed superiors*
> [4] *would be obeying orders rather than giving them*

"The theme of The Merchant *is the interdependence of human beings in civilised society. It runs like a thread through the play, showing itself in the dependence of Bassanio upon Antonio, of Gratiano upon his friends, of Old Gobbo upon Lancelot, of Lorenzo upon Jessica … All the sympathetic characters are shown as living in happy human interdependence … All who arrogate to themselves wealth or merit (not only Shylock, but the braggart Princes of Morocco and Arragon) come to woe."*

Max Plowman, *Money and* The Merchant, 1931

Having no doubts about his own worth, and confident that he deserves the hand of Portia, the Prince makes his decision. He chooses the silver casket. Inside the casket, however, there is no portrait of Portia, but a fool's head. Along with it is a scroll mocking the reader for his folly and self-delusion:

> ... Some there be that shadows kiss;
> Such have but a shadow's bliss.
> There be fools alive iwis[1]
> Silvered o'er, and so was this.[2]
>
> [1] *certainly, in truth*
> [2] *covered in silver, just as this fool's head is*

Shocked and mortified, the Prince of Arragon makes a hasty exit. Portia is relieved that yet another unsuitable admirer has, through his methodical but flawed reasoning, managed to make the wrong choice. Her waiting-woman, equally thankful, believes that these important matters are in the hands of a higher power:

Portia: Thus hath the candle singed the moth.
O, these deliberate[1] fools! When they do choose,
They have the wisdom by their wit to lose.[2]
Nerissa: The ancient saying is no heresy:[3]
'Hanging and wiving[4] goes by destiny.'

[1] *calculating*
[2] *the little insight that they have is enough to lead them to the wrong conclusions*
[3] *is a sound doctrine*
[4] *marrying*

A messenger suddenly appears: yet another suitor is on his way. The man's approach has been heralded by his companion, a young Venetian who brings both kind words and rich gifts. The suitor's name is not mentioned, but Nerissa fervently prays that the man in question is the handsome and eminently suitable Bassanio.

Shylock's grievances

Back in Venice, Salanio and Salarino are discussing the latest rumours. It seems likely that Antonio has, as they had feared, lost a valuable cargo in the English Channel:

> *Salanio:* Now, what news on the Rialto? [1]
>
> *Salarino:* Why, yet it lives there unchecked[2] that Antonio hath a ship of rich lading wracked[3] on the narrow seas.

> [1] *the traders' meeting-place in Venice*
> [2] *there is a rumour that no one has denied*
> [3] *a richly loaded ship of Antonio's has been wrecked*

Shylock now comes into view. They question him about the latest events, but he has other things on his mind. He confronts the two men angrily, convinced that they knew in advance about his daughter's elopement, but they respond by mocking him.

When they ask about Antonio, Shylock is scornful. It is not surprising that the merchant is afraid to show his face in public, he remarks. The young man needs to remember the terms of their agreement:

> *Salarino:* But tell us, do you hear whether Antonio have had any loss at sea or no?
>
> *Shylock:* There I have another bad match:[1] a bankrupt, a prodigal,[2] who dare scarce show his head on the Rialto, a beggar that was used to come so smug upon the mart.[3] Let him look to his bond.[4] He was wont to[5] call me usurer; let him look to his bond.

> [1] *poor transaction, bad deal*
> [2] *waster, profligate*
> [3] *market-place, exchange*
> [4] *he had better remind himself of our contract*
> [5] *he used to*

Shylock insists that he will not hesitate to enforce his right to a pound of flesh if the loan is not repaid. When Salarino questions why he should do such a thing, he makes it clear that he desires vengeance for years of abuse from the young merchant:

> *Shylock:* ... if it will feed nothing else, it will feed my revenge. He hath disgraced me[1] and hindered me half a million,[2] laughed at my losses, mocked at my gains, scorned my nation,[3] thwarted my bargains, cooled my friends, heated mine enemies ...
>
> [1] *insulted me in public*
> [2] *cost me half a million ducats by obstructing my business dealings*
> [3] *my people, the Jews*

The motive behind Antonio's continual harassment is simple, declares Shylock. However, the merchant is mistaken if he imagines that Shylock is anything less than human:

> *Shylock:* ... what's his reason? I am a Jew. Hath not a Jew eyes? Hath not a Jew hands, organs, dimensions, senses, affections, passions? Fed with the same food, hurt with the same weapons, subject to the same diseases, healed by the same means, warmed and cooled by the same winter and summer as a Christian is?

"Shakespeare's literary contemporaries clearly believed the anti-Semitic propaganda around them and contributed to it themselves ... With such entrenched anti-Semitism evident in Elizabethan and Jacobean society, it is interesting that, in contrast to Marlowe and Donne, Shakespeare seems to suggest that if the Jew is a monster, it is because the Christian population around him have treated him as such."

Aviva Dautch, *A Jewish Reading of* The Merchant of Venice, 2016

It is only logical, then, that Shylock will behave just as a Christian would if persecuted in the same way:

Shylock: If you prick us do we not bleed? If you tickle us do we not laugh? If you poison us do we not die? And if you wrong us shall we not revenge? If we are like you in the rest, we will resemble you in that.

Mixed emotions

A messenger from Antonio now arrives. The merchant wishes to talk to Salarino and Salanio but, as Shylock mentioned, he is unwilling to appear in public at the moment.

As the two friends leave with the messenger, Shylock's friend Tubal approaches. He has just come back from Genoa, where he has been searching for Shylock's daughter. Although Tubal has heard several reports of Jessica, he has not succeeded in finding her. Shylock is still burning with indignation at her disappearance with so much of his money and jewellery. She deserves to die for her betrayal:

Shylock: A diamond gone cost me two thousand ducats in Frankfurt ... I would my daughter were dead at my foot, and the jewels in her ear; would she were hearsed[1] at my foot, and the ducats in her coffin.

[1] *laid out for burial*

To make matters worse, Shylock has spent a substantial sum on trying to find her, to no avail. As he laments his misfortunes, Tubal mentions that he heard of another man's troubles while he was in Genoa: one of Antonio's ships has sunk in the Mediterranean.

Shylock is delighted. It seems certain that Antonio will be unable to repay his loan, and the prospect of obtaining his pound of flesh seems closer than ever. As well as taking his revenge, Shylock will remove a competitor, as Antonio has frequently lent money in the past without charging interest. He asks Tubal to help him to prepare for the merchant's arrest:

Shylock: Go, Tubal, fee me an officer;[1] bespeak him a fortnight before.[2] I will have the heart of him if he forfeit,[3] for, were he out of Venice, I can make what merchandise I will.[4]

> [1] *hire a legal officer for me*
> [2] *engage his services a fortnight before the debt is due to be repaid*
> [3] *I will have Antonio's heart if he fails to pay*
> [4] *I can drive whatever bargains I please*

Bassanio distrusts appearances   III, ii

Bassanio has arrived at Portia's home in Belmont. He has decided to take the test set by Portia's father, and choose between the three caskets. Portia is anxious. Although she denies it, she has fallen in love with him, and is afraid he may choose the wrong casket:

Portia: I pray you tarry. Pause a day or two
Before you hazard, for in choosing wrong
I lose your company; therefore, forbear awhile.
There's something tells me – but it is not love –
I would not lose you …

Unable to contain her anxiety, Portia agonises at length over her dilemma. She knows which casket Bassanio should choose, and is desperate for him to make the right choice; but to reveal it would break her promise to her dead father.

For his part, Bassanio is keen to take the test immediately. If he does not do so, another suitor might win her hand, a prospect that he finds intolerable:

Bassanio: Let me choose,
For, as I am, I live upon the rack.[1]
Portia: Upon the rack, Bassanio? Then confess
What treason there is mingled with your love.
Bassanio: None but that ugly treason of mistrust,
Which makes me fear th'enjoying of my love.[2]

    [1] *instrument of torture*
    [2] *makes me afraid that I may not win the love*
     I hope to enjoy

As Bassanio approaches the caskets, Portia orders her musicians to play a song. In her state of intense emotion, she sees her admirer as a hero going into battle:

Portia: Go, Hercules!
Live thou, I live.[1] With much, much more dismay [2]
I view the fight, than thou that mak'st the fray.[3]

    [1] *if you win, I will win*
    [2] *terror*
    [3] *lead the charge*

The song is of love, but it implies that obsessive desire based on appearance is short-lived:

Tell me where is fancy[1] bred ...
It is engendered[2] in the eye,
With gazing fed, and fancy dies
In the cradle where it lies.

    [1] *infatuation*
    [2] *created, born*

Listening to the song, Bassanio reflects that superficial beauty and refinement can disguise wickedness in many walks of life. In a law court, for example, a case may be argued elegantly even if it is morally worthless:

Bassanio: So may the outward shows be least themselves: [1]
The world is still deceived with ornament. [2]
In law, what plea so tainted and corrupt,
But, being seasoned with a gracious voice,
Obscures the show of evil?

> [1] *appearances may hide the true nature of what lies within*
> [2] *people are continually deceived by external embellishment*

In religion and in military life as well, he ponders, there are countless examples of individuals whose outward behaviour masks an ungodly or cowardly nature. Personal beauty, too, is notoriously deceptive. An attractive head of hair may have dubious origins:

Bassanio: So are those crisped[1] snaky golden locks,
Which maketh such wanton gambols with the wind
Upon supposed fairness,[2] often known
To be the dowry of a second head,[3]
The skull that bred them in the sepulchre.[4]

> [1] *curled*
> [2] *which dance so seductively in the wind on the head of a supposedly beautiful woman*
> [3] *another woman's possession*
> [4] *tomb*

"Arragon and Morocco fail because they try to interpret the lines inscribed on the caskets rather than the substance ... what they are really concerned with is themselves and the object of their suit. The noteworthy thing about Bassanio is that he disregards the inscriptions; he lets the metals themselves speak to him."

Sigurd Burckhardt, *The Gentle Bond*, 1962

Bassanio comes to a decision. The outward splendour of the gold and silver caskets cannot be trusted. He chooses instead the plain lead casket, with its inscription that demands boldness rather than promising a reward:

Bassanio: ... thou, thou meagre[1] lead,
Which rather threaten'st than dost promise aught,[2]
Thy paleness moves me more than eloquence,
And here choose I ...

[1] *lowly, worthless*
[2] *which threatens rather than promising anything*

Portia, knowing that Bassanio has chosen the right casket, can hardly contain her joy and relief.

Declarations of love

Bassanio opens the casket to reveal a portrait of his beloved. He gazes at it admiringly, then reads the scroll contained in the casket. It confirms that Portia is his:

You that choose not by the view[1]
Chance as fair and choose as true.[2]
Since this fortune falls to you,
Be content and seek no new.
If you be well pleased with this
And hold your fortune for your bliss,
Turn you where your lady is,
And claim her with a loving kiss.

[1] *who do not choose by what is outwardly visible*
[2] *have good luck that matches your wisdom*

Bassanio, almost unable to believe that he has been successful, is stunned. He kisses Portia tenderly, and she assures him that she will indeed be his wife.

For his sake, says, Portia, she wishes that she were far better, richer and more beautiful than she is. However, she is young and bright, and will do everything she can to make herself worthy of his love:

> *Portia:*   You see me, Lord Bassanio, where I stand,
> Such as I am ...
> ... an unlessoned girl, unschooled, unpractised.[1]
> Happy in this, she is not yet so old
> But she may learn; happier than this,
> She is not bred so dull but she can learn.[2]
> Happiest of all is that her gentle spirit
> Commits itself to yours to be directed ...
>
> [1] *uneducated and inexperienced*
> [2] *luckily, she is young enough to learn, and*
> *even more luckily, she is clever enough to do so*

Portia announces that everything she owns will now be Bassanio's, and she gives him a ring to symbolise their union. Overwhelmed with emotion, Bassanio vows that the ring will never leave his finger as long as he lives.

Portia's maid Nerissa congratulates the couple, and Bassanio's friend Gratiano does the same. Gratiano has an unexpected request to make:

> *Gratiano:*   ... when your honours mean to solemnize
> The bargain of your faith,[1] I do beseech you
> Even at that time I may be married too.
> *Bassanio:* With all my heart, so[2] thou canst get a wife.
> *Gratiano:* I thank your lordship; you have got me one.
>
> [1] *when you decide to celebrate your loving*
> *agreement in a wedding ceremony*
> [2] *as long as, provided that*

It now emerges that Gratiano has fallen in love with Nerissa and proposed to her. She has accepted, but on condition that Bassanio should choose the right casket and marry her mistress. Now that the outcome has proved so fortunate, they both want to get married as soon as possible.

Bassanio declares that he will be delighted to share his wedding-day with his friend. In his excitement, Gratiano proposes a bet: he is willing to stake a thousand ducats on producing a son before Bassanio and Portia.

News from Venice

Some unexpected guests now arrive. They are the two runaway lovers, Lorenzo and Jessica, now married, accompanied by Salerio, a messenger from Venice. Gratiano and Bassanio are delighted to see their Venetian friends, and welcome them warmly.

Lorenzo explains that he and Jessica had not planned this visit; however, Salerio had met them and insisted that they come with him to Belmont. Salerio confirms this, handing a letter to Bassanio. The letter is from Antonio, and Salerio hints that it may contain bad news:

> *Bassanio:*　　　　　　　　　Ere I ope[1] his letter,
> 　　　　I pray you tell me how my good friend doth.
> *Salerio:*　Not sick, my lord, unless it be in mind,[2]
> 　　　　Nor well, unless in mind.[3] His letter there
> 　　　　Will show you his estate.[4]

> [1] *open*
> [2] *apart from his mental state*
> [3] *unless he remains mentally resilient*
> [4] *condition*

Bassanio turns pale as he reads the letter. Portia insists on knowing its contents; now that their destiny is to be together, he must share his worries with her.

Bassanio first reminds her that he has never claimed to be wealthy; although of noble birth, he has not made a secret of being poor. He now confesses that he has not been telling her the whole truth.

He has in fact been living on borrowed money, he admits, and the friend who has taken responsibility for the debt, Antonio, is in terrible trouble:

Bassanio: When I told you
            My state was nothing,[1] I should then have told you
            That I was worse than nothing; for, indeed,
            I have engaged[2] myself to a dear friend,
            Engaged my friend to his mere[3] enemy,
            To feed my means.[4]

            [1] *I had no financial standing; I had no money*
            [2] *indebted, bound*
            [3] *absolute*
            [4] *sustain me in pursuing my goal*

The letter reveals that all his friend's ships have come to grief, with the loss of their valuable cargoes. Antonio is bankrupt. The date for the repayment of the loan is past, and he must face the penalty for defaulting on the debt.

Despite pleas from all the merchants and nobles of Venice, Shylock is insisting that he must have his pound of flesh, as set out in their contract. Jessica, who has heard her father discuss the matter with his friends, knows that Shylock is determined to punish Antonio. She is pessimistic about the young merchant's prospects:

Jessica: When I was with him, I have heard him swear …
           That he would rather have Antonio's flesh
           Than twenty times the value of the sum
           That he did owe him …

When Portia realises the strength of the friendship between Bassanio and Antonio, she is determined to help. She decides that, after a brief wedding ceremony, Bassanio and Gratiano must hurry back to Venice, taking enough of Portia's gold to pay off the debt many times over.

Portia asks Bassanio to read out his friend's letter, and is deeply moved. It reveals that Antonio expects to die. Any debt that Bassanio owes him is cancelled; all he asks of his friend is that, if possible, he should pay him one last visit.

Hearing this, Portia is more determined than ever to resolve the matter and save Antonio's life. Bassanio must set off as soon as possible.

A final plea
III, iii

Antonio has been arrested and imprisoned for failure to pay his debt. Escorted by his jailer, he has come to see Shylock to plead for mercy. The moneylender refuses to listen, demanding that their contract – that Antonio should forfeit a pound of flesh if he defaults – must be enforced. Antonio has frequently insulted him, and his punishment is no more than he deserves:

Shylock: Jailer, look to him.[1] Tell not me of mercy.
This is the fool that lent out money gratis.[2]
Jailer, look to him.
Antonio: Hear me yet, good Shylock.
Shylock: I'll have my bond. Speak not against my bond;
I have sworn an oath that I will have my bond.
Thou call'dst me dog before thou hadst a cause,[3]
But, since I am a dog, beware my fangs.

[1] *deal with him; take him back to prison*
[2] *without charging interest*
[3] *before you had any reason to do so*

Shylock is annoyed with the jailer for allowing his prisoner to make this visit. There is no question of relenting or giving in to the pleas of Antonio and his fellow Christians. His decision is final: he will have his pound of flesh. With that, he walks off, warning the others not to follow.

Antonio's friend Salanio, who has accompanied him, tries to comfort him. The Duke of Venice will not allow such a punishment to take place, he assures him. Antonio disagrees. Venice is an important centre of international trade, and its reputation will suffer if the law is not seen to be respected:

> *Salanio:*   I am sure the Duke
> Will never grant this forfeiture to hold.[1]
> *Antonio:* The Duke cannot deny the course of law;
> For the commodity[2] that strangers[3] have
> With us in Venice, if it be denied,
> Will much impeach the justice of the state,[4]
> Since that the trade and profit of the city
> Consisteth of all nations.

> [1] *allow this penalty to proceed*
> [2] *rights and benefits*
> [3] *foreigners, outsiders*
> [4] *would call Venetian justice into question if the law were not allowed to take its course*

Resigned to his fate, Antonio is taken back to prison. He has only one wish: that he should see his friend Bassanio before he dies in payment of his final debt.

"The roles of Antonio and Shylock, bound by their stories and by their mutual hatred, give the play its peculiar flavor. Comedy explores and celebrates society, presents us with images of harmony and community; but at the center of this comedy are two desperately solitary figures."

Levi Fox, *The Shakespeare Handbook*, 1987

A new role for Portia

The double wedding of Bassanio to Portia, and Gratiano to Nerissa, has taken place, and the two men have set off at once to help their friend in Venice. Lorenzo and Jessica, meanwhile, remain in Belmont. Lorenzo praises Portia for her steadfastness in supporting her new husband, and assures her that Bassanio's friend Antonio is a worthy recipient of the help she is offering.

Portia has never met Antonio, but is certain that, as Bassanio's close friend, he must be an admirable gentleman. She is happy, then, to help him escape from the dreadful situation that he now faces:

> *Portia:*   … in companions
> That do converse and waste the time together,
> Whose souls do bear an equal yoke of love,[1]
> There must be needs a like proportion
> Of lineaments, of manners and of spirit;[2]
> Which makes me think that this Antonio,
> Being the bosom lover of my lord,
> Must needs be like my lord. If it be so,
> How little is the cost I have bestowed
> In purchasing the semblance of my soul[3]
> From out the state of hellish cruelty.

[1] *are bound together by the love that they both feel*
[2] *there must inevitably be similarities in their physical qualities, their behaviour and their temperaments*
[3] *the money I have spent in rescuing a man who is so similar to my soulmate*

Portia now announces that she and Nerissa have vowed, while their husbands are away, to spend their time in prayer and contemplation at a nearby monastery. She asks Lorenzo to take charge of her house while she is away, and he agrees readily.

When Lorenzo and Jessica leave, however, it becomes clear that Portia has a different plan in mind. She instructs her servant Balthazar to take an urgent letter to her relative in Mantua, the illustrious lawyer Doctor Bellario. On reading the letter, the doctor will supply him with various papers and garments: Balthazar must take these, as quickly as possible, to the port. He is to meet her at the dockside where the ferry leaves for Venice.

Balthazar hurries away, and Portia now tells Nerissa that they will see their husbands sooner than expected. She does not reveal her plan, but says that it will involve disguising themselves as men. She can see herself already, outdoing her companion in her youthful bravado:

Portia: I'll hold thee any wager,
When we are both accoutred [1] like young men,
I'll prove the prettier fellow of the two,
And wear my dagger with the braver grace,
And speak between the change of man and boy
With a reed voice [2] ...

[1] *dressed*
[2] *speak with a thin, high-pitched voice, like an adolescent boy*

The name Portia inevitably brings to mind the powerful, tragic figure of Brutus's wife in *Julius Caesar*:

"Portia is a name that evokes strength and initiative in Shakespeare. The Roman Portia was the daughter of the hero of the Republic, Marcus Porcius Cato, who ultimately committed suicide rather than submitting to Caesar ... The heroine of Merchant of Venice *has the same admirable qualities of strength and determination as the Roman Portia."*

Alison Findlay, *Women in Shakespeare*, 2014

In her enthusiasm, Portia is soon carried away with the idea of playing the part of a boastful young man. She already has some detailed ideas about how she will act in her new role:

Portia: … speak of frays [1]
Like a fine bragging youth, and tell quaint lies
How honourable ladies sought my love,
Which I denying,[2] they fell sick and died.
I could not do withal; [3] then I'll repent,
And wish, for all that, that I had not killed them.
And twenty of these puny [4] lies I'll tell,
That men shall swear I have discontinued school
Above a twelvemonth. [5]

[1] *fights*
[2] *when I rejected them*
[3] *there was nothing I could do about it; it wasn't my fault*
[4] *feeble, petty*
[5] *I finished school at least a year ago*

Coming back to reality, Portia urges Nerissa to hurry away with her: a coach is waiting for them outside. They must head for the port at once.

A happy couple   III, v

In the garden outside Portia's home, Lancelot Gobbo, who came to Belmont with his new master Bassanio, is discussing his concerns with Jessica. He is worried, in his confused way, that her soul is in danger:

Lancelot: Yes, truly, for, look you, the sins of the father are
to be laid upon the children; therefore, I promise
you, I fear [1] you. I was always plain with you, and
so now I speak of my agitation of the matter.
Therefore be of good cheer, for, truly, I think you
are damned.

[1] *fear for*

Her only hope, he suggests, is that Shylock is not her real father. That would not be much of a consolation, replies Jessica light-heartedly. In any case, she no longer follows her father's religion:

Lancelot: There is but one hope in it that can do you any
good, and that is but a kind of bastard hope neither [1]
... you may partly hope that your father got you
not,[2] that you are not the Jew's daughter.

Jessica: That were a kind of bastard hope indeed, so the sins
of my mother should be visited upon me.

Lancelot: Truly, then, I fear you are damned both by father
and mother ...

Jessica: I shall be saved by my husband; he hath made me
a Christian.

[1] *it's a very weak hope at that*
[2] *didn't beget you, wasn't your father*

Lorenzo comes out into the garden and eventually persuades Lancelot to go in and prepare dinner. Alone with Jessica, he asks her opinion of Portia. She is effusive in her praise:

Lorenzo: How cheer'st thou, Jessica?
And now, good sweet, say thy opinion:
How dost thou like the Lord Bassanio's wife?

Jessica: Past all expressing.[1] It is very meet [2]
The Lord Bassanio live an upright life,
For, having such a blessing in his lady,
He finds the joys of heaven here on earth ...

[1] *more than I can say*
[2] *appropriate, right*

Bassanio should consider himself fortunate, says Jessica. Lorenzo claims, teasingly, that Jessica has been just as fortunate in having him for a husband. Jessica replies that it will be up to her to make that judgement; with that, they go in to dinner.

> "It has often been observed that Shakespeare's plays are steeped in the law. As a man of property, he knew the intricacies and technical terms of property law: language from this semantic field duly appears across the plays and poems. The case of Shylock v. Antonio in The Merchant of Venice ... is one of his great theatrical set-pieces, in which a legal nicety provides the dramatic coup."
>
> Jonathan Bate, *Soul of the Age*, 2008

Shylock remains adamant   IV, i

The day has come for Antonio to stand trial for failing to repay his loan. He is in the dock in a crowded courtroom, with nobles, attendants and officers looking on. Bassanio and Gratiano are present, too, hoping to save their friend from the penalty that Shylock has demanded.

The Duke of Venice is overseeing proceedings, and starts by expressing his sympathy for Antonio. His adversary has shown no trace of mercy, and is determined that the law should take its course without compromise.

Antonio thanks the Duke, knowing that he has done everything he can to change Shylock's mind, but assures him that he is resigned to his fate:

> *Antonio:*   ... since he stands obdurate,
> And that no lawful means can carry me
> Out of his envy's reach,[1] I do oppose
> My patience to his fury, and am armed
> To suffer[2] with a quietness of spirit,
> The very tyranny and rage of his.
>
> [1] *there is no legal way of escaping his malice*
> [2] *endure*

Shylock is called into the courtroom. The Duke proclaims that he, like everyone, expects to see a demonstration of mercy today.

The Duke believes that Shylock has knowingly brought the situation to a dramatic climax, but cannot possibly want the outcome of the trial to be fatal. Accordingly, he should not only waive his legal right to a pound of Antonio's flesh; given the huge losses that the merchant has recently suffered, he should cancel part of the debt, demanding only half of the sum originally loaned.

Shylock remains unmoved. He has made his vow; besides, the law is on his side, and if it is not followed the freedom and independence of Venice will be at risk:

> Shylock: ... by our holy Sabbath have I sworn
> To have the due and forfeit of my bond.[1]
> If you deny it, let the danger light
> Upon your charter and your city's freedom!

> [1] *the payment due to me according to our contract*

Shylock insists that he is under no obligation to explain why he has chosen to claim his pound of flesh rather than accept repayment of his loan. People behave in irrational ways all the time, he points out, but they do not have to account for their actions and feelings. His animosity towards Antonio is the only justification he is prepared to offer:

> Shylock: ... So can I give no reason, nor I will not,
> More than a lodged [1] hate and a certain loathing
> I bear Antonio, that I follow thus
> A losing suit [2] against him! Are you answered?

> [1] *deep-seated*
> [2] *an unprofitable case*

Bassanio is enraged, but Shylock responds sharply. If wrongdoing is dealt with decisively, it will not happen a second time:

Bassanio: This is no answer, thou unfeeling man,
      To excuse the current of thy cruelty!
Shylock: I am not bound to please thee with my answers.
Bassanio: Do all men kill the things they do not love?
Shylock: Hates any man the thing he would not kill? [1]
Bassanio: Every offence is not a hate at first! [2]
Shylock: What, wouldst thou have a serpent sting thee twice?

> [1] *does any man hate something and not want to kill it?*
> [2] *it is not true that every hurtful action springs from hatred*

There is no point in trying to reason with Shylock, says Antonio: it is like questioning a wolf as to why he has stolen a lamb from its mother. He asks for the trial to be concluded quickly, and for Shylock to exact his punishment.

At this point Bassanio approaches Shylock and places six thousand ducats in front of him, twice the sum originally borrowed. Shylock rejects the offer without hesitation:

Shylock: If every ducat in six thousand ducats
      Were in six parts, and every part a ducat,
      I would not draw [1] them; I would have my bond!
Duke: How shalt thou hope for mercy, rendering [2] none?
Shylock: What judgement shall I dread, doing no wrong?

> [1] *take, receive*
> [2] *giving, offering*

Many Venetians possess slaves, points out Shylock. If told to treat them more humanely or to set them free, their owners will reply that the slaves are theirs to treat as they like; they have paid for them. It is the same with his bond:

Shylock: The pound of flesh which I demand of him
Is dearly bought; 'tis mine, and I will have it.
If you deny me, fie upon your law: [1]
There is no force in the decrees of Venice.

[1] *your law is worthless*

The Duke announces that he has sent for a legal expert, Doctor Bellario, to help adjudicate on this case. He may dismiss the court if the doctor does not arrive today. At this moment news is brought into the courtroom: a messenger from Doctor Bellario himself has just arrived. The Duke orders that the messenger be summoned to the court.

The classification of *The Merchant of Venice* as a comedy is often questioned; a few critics consider it to be one of Shakespeare's 'problem plays'. Writing over three hundred years ago, one of the first scholars to produce a complete edition of Shakespeare's plays had his doubts:

"Tho' we have seen the Play Receiv'd and Acted as a Comedy, and the Part of the Jew perform'd by an Excellent Comedian, yet I cannot but think it was design'd Tragically by the Author. There appears in it such a deadly Spirit of Revenge, such a savage Fierceness and Fellness, and such a bloody designation of Cruelty and Mischief, as cannot agree either with the Stile or Characters of Comedy."

Nicholas Rowe, *The Works of William Shakespear*, 1709

Two strangers arrive

As Doctor Bellario's messenger is ushered in, Bassanio tries to reassure his friend. He will give his own life, he promises, rather than let Antonio come to harm. In his despondency, however, Antonio believes his fate is inevitable:

Antonio: I am a tainted wether [1] of the flock,
Meetest [2] for death; the weakest kind of fruit
Drops earliest to the ground, and so let me.

[1] *sickly sheep*
[2] *most suitable*

Unbeknown to those in the courtroom, the doctor's messenger is in fact Nerissa, disguised as a young man. She is dressed as a lawyer's clerk, wearing garments obtained earlier from the doctor himself. She greets the Duke and presents him with a letter from Bellario.

As the Duke peruses the letter, Shylock starts sharpening his knife as he prepares to carry out Antonio's sentence. Gratiano denounces him angrily, but to no avail:

Gratiano: ... no metal can,
No, not the hangman's axe, bear half the keenness
Of thy sharp envy. [1] Can no prayers pierce thee?
Shylock: No, none that thou hast wit enough to make.
Gratiano: O, be thou damned, inexecrable [2] dog ...
... thy desires
Are wolvish, bloody, starved and ravenous.
Shylock: Till thou canst rail the seal from off my bond [3]
Thou but offend'st thy lungs [4] to speak so loud.

[1] *not even the executioner's axe can be half as sharp as your malice*
[2] *unspeakably evil*
[3] *until your ranting can remove the seal from my contract*
[4] *you are only damaging your lungs*

The Duke now reads Doctor Bellario's letter to the court. In it, the doctor explains that he is currently in poor health, and cannot attend the hearing. He has sent another lawyer, a bright young man named Doctor Balthazar, in his place.

The two of them have already given Shylock's case a great deal of thought. Doctor Bellario assures the Duke that Balthazar is extremely wise and knowledgeable, and despite his youth is well qualified to pass judgement on the case:

> I acquainted him with the cause in controversy between the Jew and Antonio the merchant. We turned o'er [1] many books together; he is furnished with my opinion, which, bettered with his own learning, the greatness whereof I cannot enough commend, comes with him at my importunity to fill up your grace's request in my stead. [2] I beseech you, let his lack of years be no impediment ...

> [1] *consulted, scrutinised*
> [2] *at my urging he comes to the court, supplied with my opinion as well as his own, to take my place and fulfil your grace's request*

The Duke calls for Doctor Balthazar. Portia, dressed as an eminent lawyer, enters the courtroom.

"... in its eliciting of audience sympathy the play is balanced on a knife-edge: to side with the Venetians is to uphold anti-Semitic prejudice, while to sympathize with the plight of the Jew as victim is to threaten the play's formal comic ethos."

John Drakakis, Arden Shakespeare edition of *The Merchant of Venice*, 2010

An appeal for compassion

Portia starts by confirming the facts of the case with Shylock and Antonio. At first sight the situation is very simple, she declares. If Antonio is to survive, Shylock must show mercy. He cannot be forced to do so, Portia accepts, but this would be to the benefit of all concerned:

Portia: Then must the Jew be merciful.
Shylock: On what compulsion must I? Tell me that.
Portia: The quality of mercy is not strained: [1]
It droppeth as the gentle rain from heaven
Upon the place beneath. It is twice blest:
It blesseth him that gives and him that takes.

[1] *no one can be compelled to show mercy*

Portia goes on to assert that mercy is an essential attribute in those who wield power:

Portia: 'Tis mightiest in the mightiest; it becomes [1]
The thronèd monarch better than his crown.
His sceptre shows the force of temporal [2] power,
The attribute to awe and majesty,
Wherein doth sit the dread and fear of kings.
But mercy is above this sceptred sway; [3]
It is enthroned in the hearts of kings,
It is an attribute to God himself,
And earthly power doth then show likest [4] God's
When mercy seasons [5] justice.

[1] *befits*
[2] *worldly*
[3] *power demonstrated by possession of the sceptre*
[4] *most resemble*
[5] *tempers, moderates*

It droppeth as the gentle rain from heaven ...

Time and again we find in Shakespeare phrases, ideas and images drawn, consciously or unconsciously, from the Bible, a book with which he was undoubtedly very familiar.

"O howe faire a thyng is mercy in the tyme of anguish and trouble: it is like a cloud of rayne that commeth in the tyme of drought."

Ecclesiasticus Chapter 35, Geneva Bible, 1576

Turning directly to Shylock, Portia points out that through justice alone, without God's mercy, no one would deserve to go to heaven. The fact that we all desire mercy should encourage us to show it too:

Portia: Therefore, Jew,
Though justice be thy plea, consider this:
That in the course of justice none of us
Should see salvation.[1] We do pray for mercy,
And that same prayer doth teach us all to render
The deeds of mercy.[2]

[1] *if justice ran its true course, no one would escape damnation*
[2] *to act mercifully ourselves*

In summary, says Portia, if Shylock does not show mercy, the court will have no option but to allow Antonio to be put to death.

Hopes fade for Antonio

Shylock is immovable. He demands that the law must be followed, and will accept responsibility for his actions. Portia asks whether Shylock has been offered full repayment of his loan. Bassanio confirms that he has offered much more; in fact, he will give the Jew as much as he wants.

Shylock's refusal to accept the money shows that he is motivated purely by malice, maintains Bassanio. He appeals to the Duke to bend the law a little so that Antonio's life can be spared. Before the Duke can answer, Doctor Balthazar intervenes; this is out of the question, he explains. Shylock is delighted with the young man's judgement:

> *Bassanio:*   [*to the Duke*] ... I beseech you,
>   Wrest once the law to your authority; [1]
>   To do a great right, do a little wrong
>   And curb this cruel devil of his will.
> *Portia:*   It must not be: there is no power in Venice
>   Can alter a decree established.
>   'Twill be recorded for a precedent,
>   And many an error by the same example
>   Will rush into the state. [2] It cannot be.
> *Shylock:*   A Daniel [3] come to judgement; yea, a Daniel!
>   O, wise young judge, how I do honour thee.

> [1] *on this one occasion, use your power to stretch the law*
> [2] *this precedent would lead to a flood of miscarriages of justice in Venice*
> [3] *an Old Testament character renowned for his wisdom and righteousness*

Portia asks to see the contract between Antonio and Shylock, and she confirms that it is valid. Having failed to repay his debt, Antonio must forfeit a pound of flesh, to be cut out by Shylock from around his heart.

Yet again Portia asks Shylock to relent and accept a substantial payment instead of the pound of flesh; yet again he refuses. Antonio pleads for the trial to be over as soon as possible:

Shylock: By my soul I swear,
              There is no power in the tongue of man
              To alter me. I stay here on my bond.[1]
Antonio: Most heartily I do beseech the court
              To give the judgement.
Portia: Why then, thus it is:
              You must prepare your bosom for his knife.
Shylock: O noble judge! O excellent young man!

              [1] *I stand firm in demanding the fulfilment of*
              my contract

Portia calls for a set of scales to weigh the pound of flesh; Shylock has them immediately to hand. When it is suggested that a physician should be made available, Shylock makes a show of scrutinising the contract before rejecting the idea:

Portia: Have by some surgeon, Shylock, on your charge,[1]
              To stop[2] his wounds, lest he do bleed to death.
Shylock: Is it so nominated in the bond?
Portia: It is not so expressed, but what of that?
              'Twere good you do so much for charity.
Shylock: I cannot find it; 'tis not in the bond.

              [1] *under your command*
              [2] *bind, dress*

Portia asks Antonio if he has any final words. He says farewell to his dear friend Bassanio, asking him not to grieve; perhaps it will be a blessing to die, now that all his investments have failed, rather than live out the rest of his life in poverty.

Unaware of Doctor Balthazar's true identity, Antonio asks Bassanio to tell his new wife of the love that existed between the two friends. Antonio does not regret the fact that he secured the loan, he says, and neither should Bassanio:

Antonio: Repent but you[1] that you shall lose your friend
And he repents not that he pays your debt.
For if the Jew do cut but deep enough
I'll pay instantly with all my heart.

[1] *you should only be sorry*

Overcome with emotion, Bassanio cries that he would make any sacrifice at this moment to save his friend. Doctor Balthazar sounds a more level-headed note:

Bassanio: Antonio, I am married to a wife
Which is as dear to me as life itself;
But life itself, my wife and all the world
Are not with me esteemed above thy life.
I would lose all, ay, sacrifice them all
Here to this devil,[1] to deliver[2] you.
Portia: Your wife would give you little thanks for that
If she were by[3] to hear you make the offer.

[1] *Shylock*
[2] *save, rescue*
[3] *nearby*

Gratiano is equally desperate to save Antonio. Doctor Balthazar's clerk is unimpressed:

Gratiano: I have a wife who I protest I love.
I would she were in heaven, so she could
Entreat some power to change this currish[1] Jew.
Nerissa: 'Tis well[2] you offer it behind her back,
The wish would make else an unquiet house.[3]

[1] *brutish, inhuman*
[2] *it's just as well*
[3] *otherwise your comment would create an
argumentative atmosphere at home*

Shylock, scornful of the behaviour of these Christian husbands, becomes impatient. He urges Doctor Balthazar to pronounce his sentence.

The letter of the law

As Doctor Balthazar solemnly announces his verdict, Shylock becomes increasingly animated. Knife at the ready, he is eager to carry out the sentence:

Portia: A pound of that same merchant's flesh is thine;
The court awards it, and the law doth give it.

Shylock: Most rightful judge!

Portia: And you must cut this flesh from off his breast;
The law allows it, and the court awards it.

Shylock: Most learned judge!

Shylock approaches Antonio and tells him to prepare for death. However, at the last minute the judge issues a stern warning:

Portia: Tarry[1] a little, there is something else.
This bond doth give thee here no jot of blood:
The words expressly[2] are 'a pound of flesh'.
Take then thy bond: take thou thy pound of flesh.
But in the cutting it, if thou dost shed
One drop of Christian blood, thy lands and goods
Are by the laws of Venice confiscate
Unto the state[3] of Venice.

[1] *wait*
[2] *plainly, explicitly*
[3] *seized for the public treasury*

Antonio's friends are ecstatic. Doctor Balthazar points out that it was Shylock who insisted on following the letter of the law, and Gratiano taunts him with his own words:

> Gratiano: O upright judge!
>   Mark,[1] Jew – O learned judge!
> Shylock: Is that the law?
> Portia: Thyself shall see the act,[2]
>   For, as thou urgest justice, be assured
>   Thou shalt have justice more than thou desir'st.[3]
> Gratiano: O learned judge!

> [1] *take note, pay attention*
> [2] *I shall produce the text for you*
> [3] *you will have more justice than you asked for*

Shylock is dismayed at the judgement. Realising that he cannot have his pound of flesh, he resigns himself to accepting the earlier offer of money instead.

Gratiano approaches with the gold coins, but the judge intervenes once more. Shylock has demanded justice, says Balthazar, and he must have exactly what he is owed. Without shedding blood, he must cut out exactly a pound of Antonio's flesh; the contract makes no mention of any other penalty. Even repayment of the original three thousand ducats is impossible, rules Balthazar:

> Portia: Why doth the Jew pause? Take thy forfeiture.[1]
> Shylock: Give me my principal,[2] and let me go.
> Bassanio: I have it ready for thee; here it is.
> Portia: He hath refused it in the open court;
>   He shall have merely[3] justice and his bond.

> [1] *your penalty; the pound of flesh*
> [2] *the sum that I originally lent*
> [3] *purely; nothing more or less than*

> *"Paradoxically, Portia pleads eloquently for mercy, but seems merciless herself when Shylock fails to respond."*
>
> Michael Best, *Legal Comedy*, 2011

Crushed by the verdict, Shylock condemns the court angrily and turns to walk out of the courtroom. But the judge has not finished with him yet. As he has threatened the life of a Venetian citizen, Shylock is liable to lose all his property, and possibly his life as well:

Portia: Tarry, Jew,
The law hath yet another hold on you.
It is enacted in the laws of Venice,
If it be proved against an alien [1]
That by direct, or indirect, attempts
He seek the life of any citizen,
The party 'gainst the which he doth contrive [2]
Shall seize one-half his goods. The other half
Comes to the privy coffer [3] of the state,
And the offender's life lies in the mercy
Of the Duke …

[1] *foreign resident*
[2] *the person whose life has been threatened*
[3] *private treasury*

There is a clear case against Shylock, states Balthazar. His only hope is to ask the Duke for mercy. Before Shylock speaks, the Duke makes it clear that he will not seek the ultimate penalty. He may even allow the Jew to keep some of his property:

Duke: That thou shalt see the difference of our spirit, [1]
I pardon thee thy life before thou ask it.
For half thy wealth, it is Antonio's;
The other half comes to the general state,
Which humbleness may drive unto a fine. [2]

[1] *so that you will see the difference in our attitudes to justice*
[2] *which may be converted to a fine if you show repentance*

Shylock, facing financial ruin, is distraught. Antonio proposes a less drastic penalty: Shylock should keep half his property, while the half forfeited to Antonio will be held in trust and given to Lorenzo and Jessica on Shylock's death. Any property remaining in Shylock's possession when he dies must also go to the couple.

Antonio makes one further demand: that Shylock must convert to Christianity. The Duke agrees, confirming that he will reverse his decision to pardon Shylock if this requirement is not met.

Shylock agrees to Antonio's conditions without further discussion. Defeated and exhausted, he departs from the courtroom. The trial is over.

In Jonathan Miller's 1970 production of *The Merchant of Venice*, Shylock – played by Laurence Olivier – let out a long, anguished cry after he had left the courtroom.

"People have asked me about the cry that I let out offstage when Shylock exited after the court scene, mortified by the judgement. I wanted something to remain ringing in the ears long after I was in the dressing room. Something that would stay with the audience through the sweetness and light of the final romantic comic scene ... Beneath the humour there should be a sad shadow of a destroyed man. For me the cry did it."

Laurence Olivier, *On Acting*, 1986

Bassanio wavers

As Doctor Balthazar prepares to leave the courtroom, the Duke cordially invites him to dinner. The doctor declines the invitation: he must return home immediately.

Bassanio and Antonio warmly express their gratitude to the young man. The least they can do is to pay him the money that they had expected to give to Shylock. The doctor refuses, claiming that the satisfaction of doing a good job is sufficient. He hints that their paths may cross again in the future:

> *Portia:* He is well paid that is well satisfied,
> And I, delivering[1] you, am satisfied,
> And therein do account myself well paid;
> My mind was never yet more mercenary.[2]
> I pray you, know[3] me when we meet again.
> I wish you well, and so I take my leave.

> [1] *releasing, saving*
> [2] *I have never wanted any further reward than this*
> [3] *recognise, acknowledge*

If Balthazar will not accept payment, insists Bassanio, he must at least consent to have some token of their thanks. The doctor agrees to take Bassanio's gloves; then, noticing the ring he is wearing, he asks for that too.

Bassanio is taken aback, remembering how he vowed to Portia that he would never part with it under any circumstances. Doctor Balthazar is disappointed; he has taken a fancy to the ring. He is sure that Bassanio's wife would understand:

> *Portia:*   … if your wife be not a mad woman,
> And know how well I have deserved this ring,
> She would not hold out enemy[1] for ever
> For giving it to me.

> [1] *remain hostile*

When Doctor Balthazar and his clerk have left, Bassanio has second thoughts. Persuaded by Antonio, he gives the ring to Gratiano and tells him to hurry away and present it to the young man:

> *Antonio:* My lord Bassanio, let him have the ring.
> Let his deservings and my love withal
> Be valued 'gainst your wife's commandement.[1]
> *Bassanio:* Go, Gratiano, run and overtake him;[2]
> Give him the ring ...
>
> [1] *weigh what he has done for us, along with my friendship, against your wife's instruction*
> [2] *catch up with him*

Bassanio announces that the three of them will set off back to Belmont tomorrow. He and Gratiano will be reunited with their wives, and Antonio will be their guest.

A present for the judge IV, ii

Portia and Nerissa, still in disguise, are looking for Shylock's house. The judgement of the court, requiring him to surrender half his goods to Antonio and to bequeath the rest to Lorenzo and Jessica in his will, must be presented to Shylock for signature. When this is done, the two women will travel back to Belmont immediately, aiming to arrive before their husbands.

Gratiano now approaches. His friend Bassanio has changed his mind, he explains, producing the ring that previously caught Doctor Balthazar's eye. The doctor accepts it gratefully. Gratiano then offers to show the doctor's clerk the way to Shylock's house.

Nerissa takes Portia aside for a moment, and mentions that she is going to take advantage of her husband's company to see if she can persuade him, like his friend, to part with his wedding-ring.

Portia is confident that Nerissa can do it, and envisages the two men, when confronted, swearing blind that they did not give their rings away to women:

Nerissa: I'll see if I can get my husband's ring,
Which I did make him swear to keep for ever.

Portia: Thou mayst, I warrant.[1] We shall have old[2] swearing
That they did give the rings away to men,
But we'll outface them and outswear them too.[3]

[1] *you'll succeed, I bet*
[2] *endless*
[3] *we'll stand up to them, and bluster even more than they do*

Night music

V, i

Newlyweds Lorenzo and Jessica, unaware of the dramatic events unfolding in Venice, are enjoying the balmy night air in Portia's garden in Belmont. They dreamily recall the adventures of famous, tragic lovers of the past:

Lorenzo: The moon shines bright. In such a night as this,
When the sweet wind did gently kiss the trees,
And they did make no noise, in such a night
Troilus, methinks, mounted the Trojan walls
And sighed his soul toward the Grecian tents,
Where Cressid lay that night.

Jessica: In such a night
Did Thisbe fearfully o'ertrip the dew,[1]
And saw the lion's shadow ere himself,[2]
And ran dismayed[3] away.

[1] *skip nervously through the dew-covered grass*
[2] *before she saw the lion itself*
[3] *terrified*

They playfully add themselves to the list, remembering their own elopement, when Jessica escaped from her father's house with a supply of money and jewels:

Lorenzo: In such a night
Did Jessica steal[1] from the wealthy Jew,
And with an unthrift love[2] did run from Venice
As far as Belmont.

Jessica: In such a night
Did young Lorenzo swear he loved her well,
Stealing her soul with many vows of faith,
And ne'er a true one.[3]

[1] *run away; also, pilfer*
[2] *a lover who was extravagant and wasteful*
[3] *not one of which was true*

In such a night ...

The love affair between Troilus and Cressida took place during the Trojan war, when Troy was besieged by the Greeks. Cressida's father had deserted Troy and joined the Greek camp, and Cressida was later sent out to join him. Despite her promise to come back to Troilus, she fell in love with the Greek warrior Diomedes and never returned.

Pyramus and Thisbe were two Babylonian lovers who, forbidden to meet by their parents, arranged a secret rendezvous. Thisbe, arriving first, was terrified by the sight of a lion, and ran away. In her haste she lost her veil, which the lion seized in its jaws. Pyramus then arrived; seeing the lion's tracks, and Thisbe's torn, bloodied veil, he assumed the worst, and slew himself.

"Upon a moonlit bank in Belmont, Lorenzo and Jessica find, through their love for each other, a harmony that seems momentarily to put them in touch with the music of the spheres, but even as they do so they remember the stories of tragic lovers divided by misunderstanding and by death."

Levi Fox, *The Shakespeare Handbook*, 1987

The two lovers are interrupted by a messenger, Stephano, sent by Portia. He informs the couple that Portia and Nerissa are on their way back from the monastery, where they have been on a secluded religious retreat.

Lorenzo and Jessica are just about to go inside to prepare for Portia's return when another messenger arrives. This time it is Lancelot Gobbo, bellowing and whooping through the darkness. He announces that he has a message for Lorenzo. Lancelot's master Bassanio will be home tonight:

Lancelot: Tell him there's a post[1] come from my master,
with his horn full of good news. My master will
be here ere morning.

[1] *courier who announces his arrival with a hunting-horn*

Lorenzo asks Stephano to bring some musicians out into the garden, where they can play to celebrate Portia's return. Music is the perfect accompaniment to the gentle night air, he declares, as he relaxes on a grassy bank:

Lorenzo: How sweet the moonlight sleeps upon this bank!
Here we will sit, and let the sounds of music
Creep in our ears. Soft stillness and the night
Become the touches[1] of sweet harmony.

[1] *are fitting for the playing*

Looking up at the clear night sky, Lorenzo reflects that the heavens themselves produce harmonious music, inaudible to humans, as the stars follow their paths across the sky.

As the musicians start to play, Jessica remarks that she never feels merry when she hears beautiful music. Lorenzo agrees; music provokes stillness, calm and contemplation. Even wild animals, he claims, become serene and attentive when music is played.

Anyone who is indifferent to the power of music, claims Lorenzo, is likely to be corrupt and deceitful, and should be avoided at all costs:

Lorenzo: The man that hath no music in himself,
Nor is not moved with concord of sweet sounds,
Is fit for treasons, stratagems and spoils; [1]
The motions of his spirit are dull as night [2]
And his affections dark as Erebus. [3]
Let no such man be trusted.

[1] *dirty tricks and plunder*
[2] *his soul is dull and lifeless*
[3] *his feelings are as dark as the Underworld*

Return to Belmont

Portia and Nerissa, travelling homewards through the darkness, see a welcome light in the distance. The moon is now hidden behind clouds, making the light seem much brighter:

Portia: That light we see is burning in my hall.
How far that little candle throws his beams!
So shines a good deed in a naughty [1] world.

[1] *wicked*

Suddenly they hear music. Portia is enchanted: then, discovering that it is the familiar sound of her own musicians, she realises that – as with the light burning in her house – it is circumstances that heighten her appreciation:

Portia: Music, hark!
Nerissa: It is your music, madam, of the house.
Portia: Nothing is good, I see, without respect. [1]
Methinks it sounds much sweeter than by day!
Nerissa: Silence bestows that virtue on it, madam.
Portia: The crow doth sing as sweetly as the lark
When neither is attended [2] ...

[1] *consideration of its setting*
[2] *when no one is listening to judge them*

As the two women approach the house, Lorenzo greets them and mentions that their husbands are expected back shortly. Portia tells Nerissa to hurry inside and instruct the servants not to reveal that the two of them have been away. Lorenzo and Jessica too promise not to mention their absence.

A trumpet-call heralds the arrival of Bassanio's party. Overhearing Portia remark on the dim early morning light, Bassanio praises her radiant beauty:

Portia: 'Tis a day
          Such as the day is when the sun is hid.
Bassanio: We should hold day with the Antipodes,
          If you would walk in absence of the sun.[1]
Portia: Let me give light, but let me not be light;[2]
          For a light wife doth make a heavy[3] husband ...

[1] *if you walked at night-time, you would turn night
   into day, so our daytime would match that of the
   Antipodes*
[2] *wanton, immoral*
[3] *miserable*

Bassanio introduces Antonio, his beloved friend. Portia points out that he certainly deserves Bassanio's love for his selfless generosity:

Bassanio: This is the man, this is Antonio,
To whom I am so infinitely bound.[1]
Portia: You should in all sense[2] be much bound to him,
For, as I hear, he was much bound for you.[3]

[1] indebted; tied by the strong bond of friendship
[2] in every sense of the word
[3] put under a heavy obligation on your behalf

Two missing rings

Elsewhere in the garden, an argument has broken out. Nerissa has confronted her new husband Gratiano, who is vehemently defending himself. It soon becomes clear that they are quarrelling about the wedding-ring given away to Doctor Balthazar's clerk:

Gratiano: By yonder moon, I swear you do me wrong!
In faith, I gave it to the judge's clerk.
Would he were gelt[1] that had it, for my part,
Since you do take it, love, so much at heart.

[1] castrated

When Portia asks to know more, Gratiano is dismissive of the ring, with its simple, sentimental inscription. His wife reminds him of his promise:

Gratiano: ... a hoop of gold, a paltry ring
That she did give me, whose posy[1] was
For all the world like cutler's poetry[2]
Upon a knife: 'Love me and leave me not.'
Nerissa: What talk you of the posy or the value?
You swore to me when I did give it you
That you would wear it till your hour of death ...

[1] inscribed message
[2] the poetry (often very unsophisticated)
traditionally engraved on cutlery

Nerissa alleges that he has given the ring to another woman, but Gratiano insists that the recipient was a young man, hardly more than a boy. In his irritation he describes the youth in disparaging terms:

Nerissa: Gave it a judge's clerk! No, God's my judge,
            The clerk will ne'er wear hair on's face[1] that had it.
Gratiano: He will, an if[2] he live to be a man.
Nerissa: Ay, if a woman live to be a man.
Gratiano: Now, by this hand, I gave it to a youth,
            A kind of boy, a little scrubbed[3] boy,
            No higher than thyself, the judge's clerk,
            A prating[4] boy that begged it as a fee …

[1] *will never grow a beard; is not a man*
[2] *as long as*
[3] *puny, diminutive*
[4] *prattling, chattering*

Portia interrupts. She is on Nerissa's side, she maintains; after all, Gratiano had vowed faithfully to keep the ring come what may. She herself has also given a ring to her husband, and it is unthinkable that he should have given it away. Bassanio wonders desperately how he is going to explain himself:

Portia: I gave my love a ring and made him swear
            Never to part with it, and here he stands.
            I dare be sworn for him he would not leave it,[1]
            Nor pluck it from his finger, for the wealth
            That the world masters.[2] Now, in faith, Gratiano,
            You give your wife too unkind a cause of grief.
            An 'twere to me,[3] I should be mad at it.
Bassanio: [*aside*] Why, I were best to cut my left hand off
            And swear I lost the ring defending it.

[1] *I'm prepared to swear, on his behalf, that he
     would never let go of it*
[2] *for all the wealth in the world*
[3] *if this were to happen to me*

Before Bassanio can gather his thoughts, however, Gratiano, in his frustration, blurts out the truth: Bassanio, like him, has given away his ring. The rings went to the judge and his clerk after Antonio's trial, he explains. They thoroughly deserved a reward, and neither man would accept anything other than the wedding-rings.

Bassanio confirms his friend's account, holding up his hand to show that he no longer has the ring. Portia vows that she will not share a bed with Bassanio until her ring is returned, and Nerissa follows her example. Bassanio pleads fervently with Portia to change her mind, but she answers in the same vein, echoing his rhetoric:

> *Bassanio:*   Sweet Portia,
>   If you did know to whom I gave the ring,
>   If you did know for whom I gave the ring,
>   And would conceive [1] for what I gave the ring …
>   You would abate [2] the strength of your displeasure.
> *Portia:*   If you had known the virtue of the ring,
>   Or half her worthiness that gave the ring,
>   Or your own honour to contain [3] the ring,
>   You would not then have parted with the ring.
>   … I'll die for't, [4] but some woman had the ring!

> [1] *could imagine*
> [2] *reduce, moderate*
> [3] *protect, keep*
> [4] *I'm prepared to stake my life on saying it*

Bassanio, like Gratiano, insists that the ring was not given to a woman. The man who now possesses it is a highly regarded doctor of law who, despite having saved Antonio's life, refused to take any money for his services.

Portia retorts that Bassanio had better be careful: just as he has been generous in giving away the ring, she will be equally free in her own way if she meets this brilliant doctor.

Nerissa affirms that she will behave likewise, and her husband responds with jealous fury. If he discovers her with the doctor's clerk, there will be hell to pay:

Portia: Let not that doctor e'er come near my house!
Since he hath got the jewel that I loved
And that which you did swear to keep for me,
I will become as liberal as you;
I'll not deny him anything I have …
                                    … if I be left alone,
Now, by mine honour,[1] which is yet mine own,
I'll have that doctor for my bedfellow.
Nerissa: And I his clerk. Therefore be well advised
How you do leave me to mine own protection.[2]
Gratiano: Well, do you so; let not me take him then,[3]
For if I do I'll mar[4] the young clerk's pen.

[1] *chastity, virginity*
[2] *think carefully before leaving me to my own devices*
[3] *catch him with you*
[4] *spoil, break*

The Merchant of Venice was written during a particularly fruitful and busy period of Shakespeare's creative life, when he was combining the roles of writer, actor, and shareholder in London's leading theatre company:

"In London he was in the thick of things, at the beck and call of busy colleagues … messengers could fetch him to the theatre when crisis came, and his counsel was precious. Interrupted or not, the author-actor-manager was not slow in authorship … Between the beginning of 1597 and the end of 1601, Shakespeare, amid all his other duties of the playhouse, wrote The Merchant of Venice, *the two parts of* Henry IV, Love's Labour's Lost, Henry V, Much Ado about Nothing, Julius Caesar, The Merry Wives of Windsor, Troilus and Cressida, As You Like It, Twelfth Night *and* Hamlet … *Never again was there to be such a marriage of abundance with excellence."*

Ivor Brown, *How Shakespeare Spent the Day*, 1963

Happy endings

During the squabbling of the two reunited couples, their guest Antonio has been standing by quietly. At this point, aware that it was his predicament that led to the present discord, he cuts in apologetically:

> *Antonio:* I am th'unhappy subject of these quarrels.

Portia assures Antonio that he is a welcome visitor; he must not allow this marital conflict to upset him. Bassanio appeals to Portia for forgiveness, swearing that he will never again break a promise, and this time Antonio backs him up. Earlier he stood as guarantor of Bassanio's loan, and now he will do the same for his friend's trustworthiness:

> *Antonio:* I once did lend my body for his wealth,[1]
> Which, but for him that had your husband's ring,
> Had quite miscarried.[2] I dare be bound again:
> My soul upon the forfeit,[3] that your lord
> Will never more break faith advisedly.[4]

[1] *put my life at stake for his prosperity and well-being*
[2] *would have been destroyed had it not been for the doctor who now owns Bassanio's ring*
[3] *I offer my soul as a bond*
[4] *knowingly, deliberately*

Portia accepts Antonio's pledge. She then hands him a ring, instructing him to give it to her husband. Bassanio is amazed to see that it is the same ring he gave to Doctor Balthazar. However, his delight is shattered when Portia reveals that it was Balthazar who gave it to her. In fact, she has even shared a bed with the doctor.

To Gratiano's horror, Nerissa confesses that she has recovered her ring in the same way. Only last night she slept with the young clerk about whom Gratiano was so dismissive:

Bassanio: By heaven, it is the same I gave the doctor!
Portia: I had it of [1] him. Pardon me, Bassanio,
For by this ring the doctor lay with me. [2]
Nerissa: And pardon me, my gentle Gratiano,
For that same scrubbed [3] boy, the doctor's clerk,
In lieu of this, [4] last night did lie with me.
Gratiano: …What, are we cuckolds ere we have deserved it?
Portia: Speak not so grossly.

[1] from
[2] I swear by this ring that I slept with the doctor
[3] puny
[4] in exchange for this ring

Portia calmly addresses the bewildered men. She produces a letter from Doctor Bellario confirming that the fictional Doctor Balthazar was in fact Portia, while Nerissa was the doctor's clerk. Lorenzo will vouch that the two women have been away from Belmont; they have only just come back, and have not yet even set foot in the house.

However, this is not the only surprise for the group assembled in Portia's garden. She has some unexpected news for Antonio, too, and hands him a letter. It concerns the precious cargoes that he believed to have been lost at sea:

Portia: Unseal this letter soon;
There you shall find three of your argosies [1]
Are richly come to harbour suddenly. [2]

[1] trading-vessels
[2] unexpectedly

As Antonio reads the letter with amazement, his two friends turn again to their wives, hardly able to believe what has happened:

Bassanio: [*to Portia*] Were you the doctor, and I knew you not?
Gratiano: [*to Nerissa*] Were you the clerk that is to make me cuckold? [1]
Nerissa: Ay, but the clerk that never means to do it,
Unless he live until he be a man.

[1] *who intends to sleep with my wife*

Antonio joyfully announces that the letter confirms, as Portia promised, that his ships have arrived safely.

Portia now turns to Lorenzo and Jessica: they are to share in the good fortune that is coming to light in Belmont. As ordered by the court in Venice, Shylock will bequeath all his possessions to the couple on his death. Doctor Balthazar's clerk has ensured that Shylock himself has signed the agreement:

Portia: How now, Lorenzo?
My clerk hath some good comforts too for you.
Nerissa: Ay, and I'll give them him without a fee.
There do I give to you and Jessica
From the rich Jew, a special deed of gift, [1]
After his death, of all he dies possessed of.

[1] *document confirming the bequest*

"Preoccupied as they are with their reunion in Belmont, the Christians give no thought at all to Shylock whom they mention only once … It is unlikely that the audience, however, will so easily forget the ominous figure of Shylock whose defeat they have just witnessed, and we may wonder how far Shakespeare intended their disregard of that ruined man to be a silent comment on their frivolity. The dramatist may or may not invite us to read between the lines."

John Wilders, BBC TV Shakespeare edition of
The Merchant of Venice, 1980

The night is nearly over, remarks Portia; it is time to leave the garden and go inside. They all have plenty to talk about, and many questions to ask. Gratiano volunteers the first question. He wants to know Nerissa's intentions:

Gratiano: ... Whether till the next night she had rather stay,[1]
Or go to bed now, being two hours to day.[2]
But, were the day come, I should wish it dark[3]
Till I were couching[4] with the doctor's clerk!

[1] *wait*
[2] *as daylight is still two hours away*
[3] *if we were to wait, I would spend the whole day wishing night would come*
[4] *in bed*

Whatever happens, Gratiano is certain of one thing: from now on, he will take great care of Nerissa's precious wedding-ring.

―――――――
――――――

Acknowledgements

The following publications have proved invaluable as sources of factual information and critical insight:

- C. L. Barber, *The Merchants and the Jew of Venice*, from *Shakespeare's Festive Comedy*, Princeton University Press, 1959

- Jonathan Bate, *Soul of the Age*, Penguin, 2009

- Michael Best, Introduction to *The Merchant of Venice*, Internet Shakespeare Editions, University of Victoria, 2011

- Charles Boyce, *Shakespeare A to Z*, Roundtable Press, 1990

- Ivor Brown, *How Shakespeare Spent the Day*, Bodley Head, 1963

- Sigurd Burckhardt, *The Gentle Bond*, from *Journal of English Literary History*, Johns Hopkins University Press, 1962

- Aviva Dautch, *A Jewish Reading of* The Merchant of Venice, from *Discovering Literature*, British Library, 2016

- John Drakakis, Introduction to *The Merchant of Venice* in the Arden Shakespeare Third Series, 2010

- Alison Findlay, *Women in Shakespeare*, Bloomsbury Arden Shakespeare, 2014

- Nicholas Fogg, *Hidden Shakespeare*, Amberley Publishing, 2013

- Levi Fox, *The Shakespeare Handbook*, Bodley Head, 1987

- John Goodwin, Programme notes for *The Merchant of Venice*, RSC Publications, 1965

- Farah Karim-Cooper, *Questions of Value in* The Merchant of Venice, Shakespeare's Globe Trust, 2016

- Laurie Maguire and Emma Smith, *30 Great Myths About Shakespeare*, Wiley-Blackwell, 2013

- Laurence Olivier, *On Acting*, Weidenfeld & Nicolson, 1986

- Max Plowman, *Money and* The Merchant, *The Adelphi*, 1931

- Caroline Spurgeon, *Shakespeare's Imagery and What It Tells Us*, Cambridge University Press, 1935

- John Wain, *The Living World of Shakespeare*, Macmillan, 1964

- John Wilders, Introduction to *The Merchant of Venice*, BBC TV Shakespeare, 1980

All quotations from *The Merchant of Venice* are taken from the Arden Shakespeare.

Guides currently available in the *Shakespeare Handbooks* series are:

www.shakespeare-handbooks.com

www.ingramcontent.com/pod-product-compliance
Lightning Source LLC
Chambersburg PA
CBHW071829020426
42331CB00007B/1670